Homemade Root Beer Soda & Pop

Stephen Cresswell

Storey Publishing

The mission of Storey Publishing is to serve our customers by publishing practical information that encourages personal independence in harmony with the environment.

Edited by Pamela B. Lappies
Cover design by Meredith Maker
Cover photograph by Stock Food
Text design and production by Mark Tomasi
Production assistance by Jennifer Jepson
Line drawings by Randy Mosher
Indexed by Peggy Holloway

Printed in the United States by Malloy Printing
15 14 13 12 11

Library of Congress Cataloging-in-Publication Data

Cresswell, Stephen Edward.
    Homemade root beer, soda, and pop / Stephen Cresswell.
        p.   cm.
    Includes bibliographical references and index.
    ISBN-13: 978-1-58017-052-9 (pbk. : alk. paper)
    1. Carbonated beverages—Amateurs' manuals. I. Title.
TP630.C74 1998
641.8'75—dc20
                                                                        97-49254
                                                                        CIP

Contents

Preface

This book explains how root beers and other traditional soft drinks can still be made "from scratch" at home and includes a number of recipes devised especially for this volume. You'll also find a generous sprinkling of recipes dating from much earlier times, which I have been collecting for many years, culling them from old cookbooks, newspapers, and magazines. Featuring yesterday's tastes alongside today's techniques, *Homemade Root Beer, Soda, and Pop* is able to fill several needs.

First, there is an unfortunate lack of books that discuss the creation of homemade soft drinks. A few books include one or two recipes, but these are hard to find. Second, as a history teacher I enjoy delving into the past. Accumulating recipes for root beers, ginger ales, and birch beers, dating back many years, decades, and even centuries, has been a pleasurable pastime. I've found some particularly unusual recipes, such as those for Tomato Beer and Pumpkin Ale. Rather than allow these recipes to molder in dusty cookbooks and forgotten journals, I wanted to share them with people who might be interested in re-creating the potable treasures of years gone by. Finally, this book will teach techniques of brewing that are quite similar to those used in beer making, and those who choose to do so can very easily go on to add delicious homebrewed beers to their repertoire of bottled homemade beverages.

Historical Recipes in This Book

The sidebars of this book contain the word-for-word recipes written down many years ago by farm wives, amateur scientists, women journalists, and experts in home economics. I enjoy reading these recipes because they offer a rare window into what Americans were drinking with their dinner — or during the hot work of blacksmithing, threshing, or clothes washing — so long ago. Often the most valuable parts of the recipe are the little comments by the person recording it, comments that tell us of American attitudes about taste, about drinking, and even about humanity.

A Note about Historical Recipes

Nearly all of the historical recipes are from the United States, though a few from other nations are included for variety. The recipes are reproduced verbatim from the original sources with no attempt made to change or mark odd, archaic, or "incorrect" spelling or grammar. The sources for these recipes are listed on page 109.

These recipes may give you ideas for formulating new and modern ones on your own. Or you may want to try some of these recipes as written, with no variation in the ingredients. Really, though, you will obtain the best results by adhering to the modern brewing techniques outlined in chapter 3. You'll enjoy success by following the "refrigerator method" that was used in all of the modern soft drink recipes in this book. As with the modern recipes, these older recipes will benefit from the use of utensils, carboys, and bottles that have been sanitized ahead of time with hot water to which some plain chlorine bleach has been added (about 2 tablespoons of bleach per gallon of water).

Note, too, some differences in terminology. In years gone by, when a recipe called for yeast, it was expected that the cook would add a lump of bread dough (containing as it did active yeast) or a measure of beer with still-active yeast in it. Accordingly, many of the historical recipes call for half a cup or more of yeast. This would be an absurdly excessive amount using today's granulated yeast. With modern ale yeast (available from homebrew supply shops), about ⅛ teaspoon per gallon should be about right. Actually, the precise measure is really unimportant. The yeast will simply multiply until all the sugars are fermented — or until you stop the fermentation by chilling. Using more yeast than ⅛ teaspoon may cause the carbonation to proceed more quickly than you expect, however. Wine yeast or even bread yeast will work, too, in the same amounts as with ale yeast, if ale yeast isn't available.

The earliest recipes here come from the 1600s; the last of them was written down in 1939. While none of these recipes was designed to make a strong alcoholic drink, remember the basic principles of brewing to ensure that you create essentially nonalcoholic drinks if that is important to you. To make a virtually nonalcoholic drink, you should not allow the yeast and sugar to work together for more than an hour or so before bottling. Except in the case of citrus drinks, which carbonate very slowly, nonalcoholic drinks should "work" only two or three days after bottling. Move them to the refrigerator as soon as the carbonation is right. Don't allow the drinks to overcarbonate, or the alcohol in the drink might prove to go beyond trace amounts.

A Dash of Common Sense

Use common sense and your developing expertise as you read the historical recipes. Consider Mrs. Porter's 1871 recipe for Cream Beer, for example (page 6). After reading the recipe several times, you will notice something strange: The recipe calls for 2¼ pounds of sugar and less than 1 quart of liquid. Sweet drink, eh? Though Mrs. Porter doesn't say so, surely the intent was to make a concentrated drink that would then be diluted heavily with water. Once again, just use logic and your knowledge of other recipes as you read these older "receipts" from the pages of history.

Root Beers in American History

In years gone by, self-sufficiency was the goal on American farms. The small cash income went for land purchase, taxes, and a few exotic products such as coffee and cinnamon. Farm families aimed to produce their own clothes, furniture, rugs, brooms, brushes, harnesses, animal feed, and fencing. They would also strive to make and preserve virtually all food for their own use — from bread, milk, and cheese, to canned vegetables, fruit preserves, dried apples, and smoked bacon. An integral part of this self-reliance was the making and bottling of refreshing beverages for year-round use.

For many families, these beverages included wine and cider from apples, grapes, and other fruits; beer made from barley, sorghum molasses, and hops; and nonalcoholic drinks flavored with the roots, bark, sap, and leaves of local wild plants.

Traditional Methods and Ingredients

For both alcoholic and nonalcoholic brewed beverages, our forebears heated water to extract the flavor from grains, leaves, roots, flowers, and bark. Favorite flavorings for all strengths of brew included gingerroot, sassafras root, and hop flowers. One essential ingredient was some form of sugar. For stronger beers, yeasts would convert the sugar to alcohol. For both strong beers and nonintoxicating root beers, this same fermentation process resulted in carbon-dioxide gas, which carbonated the drink. Molasses was one favorite form of sugar; it was less expensive than more refined types of sugar and added a lot of flavor and color. Honey and maple sap were two other sources of sugar. In the case of stronger beers, the brewer took barley and wheat through a malting process that brought out the natural sugars in the sprouted grain.

After perhaps an hour of simmering, the watery solution (now called wort, and pronounced wert) was allowed to cool to lukewarm. Then the beverage maker added yeast, and the wort was put into a barrel or crock to ferment. If the aim was a beer with a noticeable alcohol content, the brewer let the yeast convert nearly all the sugar to alcohol. When only a little sugar remained, the beer was put into bottles and corked, and the corks were then tied down with wire. This way, the last little bit of fermentation resulted in the making and trapping of carbonation.

 Alcoholic or Nonalcoholic?

The sharp distinction modern Americans draw between alcoholic and nonalcoholic beverages was more relaxed in earlier times. Colonial farmers on the eastern seaboard knew they could make "small beers" that were low in alcohol, "table beers" that had a moderate amount of alcohol, and "strong beers" that, as the name implies, packed a wallop. If the beverage was mostly for young children, it was possible to brew a beer with only the tiniest trace of alcohol in it. In short, farm families did not think of there being two classes of beverage, alcoholic and nonalcoholic. They knew that there was a whole spectrum of strengths and flavors that could be brewed.

The steps followed in the making of essentially nonalcoholic root beers were identical, except that the bottling took place just after the yeast was added, and the fermentation was stopped after a day or two by cooling the bottles. The root beers were not truly nonalcoholic, of course, but the alcohol content was very low. (Small amounts of alcohol are also produced in the making of apple cider, bread, and other common food products.) Several million American root cellars and springhouses were filled with bottles of beverages, made from the harvest of farm and meadow.

HEALTH-GIVING WATERS

Since its earliest times, human society has been aware that certain waters seem to cause bad health, while other sources of water seem to rejuvenate people and even cure illnesses. Every society has sought out mineral waters, especially waters that sport an effervescence. The interest in mineral waters led scientists to try to produce sparkling waters in the laboratory. A Swiss alchemist named Thurneysser was among the first to try to carbonate water artificially; he conducted his experiments in 1560. European scientists finally did perfect various processes of carbonating water, involving, for example, the use of strong acids and powdered chalk, but still the easiest way to obtain a carbonated beverage was either to visit a mineral spring or to brew beer.

In the United States, mineral springs were popular among those who could afford to visit them or were fortunate enough to live near one. In 1781, while George Washington was awaiting a document relating to the surrender of the British, he visited a mineral spring to pass the time. In 1784, Colonel Othy Williams wrote to Washington about Saratoga Springs in New York, reporting that the water there was extremely carbonated. "Several persons told us that they had corked it tight in bottles, and that the bottles broke," he wrote. Williams tried the experiment himself, and while the bottles didn't break, the carbonation did push its way past a wooden cork and a wax seal to escape. Doctors were sure that if waters like those found at Saratoga Springs were widely available to all Americans, the nation would be much healthier.

American doctors, pharmacists, and scientists worked hard under primitive conditions to produce soda water artificially, to allow the manufacture of a nonalcoholic beverage that would be a tonic or a curative. Two Americans seem to have tied for the honor of being the

The Heritage of Brewing

Both men and women brewed beverages in colonial America. George Washington, Thomas Jefferson, and Benjamin Franklin have all left us their favorite recipes for small beers, persimmon beer, and other interesting beverages. Dozens of American women also wrote down their recipes, and in some cases published their favorite "receipts" in "cookery books" that sold tens of thousands of copies. Whether the drink in question was to be strong or essentially nonalcoholic, the process for making it was basically the same.

Farm families fervently believed that their beverages were good for them, since many of the herbs used in brewing had tonic or medicinal properties. Compared with the tainted water often found in shallow wells or creeks that ran through cow fields, bottled beverages were quite a bit healthier to drink. Even though the beverages were brewed from the same water, the water had been boiled. Further, even tiny amounts of alcohol have antimicrobial qualities, as do the carbon-dioxide gas and the hops. Add the healthful properties of the other ingredients (fruits and yeasts, for example) and there was a recipe for a genuinely salutary drink.

first to bottle commercially nonalcoholic carbonated beverages. In 1807, Dr. Benjamin Silliman was beginning to supply residents of New Haven, Connecticut, with carbonated soda water, but found it almost impossible to find suitable bottles. "I cannot procure any glass bottles which will not burst," Silliman wrote, "nor any stone ones which are impervious to the fixed air [carbon-dioxide gas]." Also in 1807, one Joseph Hawkins was selling bottled soda water in Philadelphia.

BIRTH OF THE SODA FOUNTAIN

The new trend was for soda-water merchants to attempt to duplicate the fancy mineral springs in an urban environment. One of the most popular new "soda fountains" was located in the Tontine Coffee House on Wall Street in New York, which opened in 1794. Another such urban watering place could be found circa 1805 at a Philadelphia saloon called the Shakespeare Gallery. One advertisement for the gallery reported that carbonated waters were on tap, and that novels, newspapers, and pamphlets were lying about, "so as to combine amusement with utility in this novel and salutary establishment." In short, the Shakespeare Gallery was intended to be "not only conducive to the health of the city, but an elegant and fashionable lounge for ladies and gentlemen throughout the day."

While such urban resorts were popular with the leisure class, it was apothecary shops that helped the masses obtain carbonated drinks. As headachey and nauseated customers dropped by the shop, the apothecary could suggest various remedies, including soda waters on tap. From sparkling water it was only a small step to flavored soft drinks. One pioneer in making nonalcoholic soft drinks was Pierre Lacour, who was living and writing in France. His research was made available to Americans in the 1868 translation *The Manufacture of Liquors, Wines, and Cordials Without the Aid of Distillation; Also the Manufacture of Effervescing Beverages and Syrups, Vinegars, and Bitters.* Lacour provided, for the use of pharmacists, recipes for various syrups made with lemon, vanilla, grape, and mulberry, and one syrup called Spirit of Aromatics, which included ginger, sassafras, cloves, lemon, and bergamot. The new procedure was for pharmacists to make up syrups in advance, then put a little into each glass as needed, fill with cold carbonated water and stir. Soon American drugstores were fitted out with marble-topped counters and stools, and a

Three Syrups for Beverages

Recipes of Pierre Lacour of France
From an English Translation published in New York, 1863

Blackberry Syrup. — Expressed juice of blackberries, one pint; clarified sugar, two and a half pounds; whiskey or brandy, half a glass. Dissolve the sugar by the aid of heat, in the juice, in the same manner as for other syrup. When the syrup is cool, add the spirit.

The juice is expressed from fruit by placing it in a bag of suitable size, and submitting it to pressure. When the juice is too thick, dilute it with water. It is customary to make a pint of syrup from a pint measure of the fruit.

Pineapple Syrup. — This can be made in the same manner as blackberry, or by slicing the fruit, alternating the slices with layers of powdered sugar, permitting them to stand twenty-four hours, and then expressing the syrup formed. Each pound of the pared fruit, with thirty ounces of sugar, should yield, with the requisite quantity of water, two pints of syrup.

These syrups will have their aromatic aroma greatly impaired by heat.

Syrup of Jessamine. — Simple syrup [of sugar and water], pint and a half; spirit of orris-root, one ounce; essence of bergamont, two drachms*; essence of lemon, one drachm; essence of cinnamon, five drops; slightly warm the syrup, and add the essences.

The preceding syrups are employed for flavoring drinks, soda water, &c.

---

*drachm: An apothecaries' unit of weight equal to 1/8 ounce. Also called a dram.

Cream Beer

Mrs. M. E. Porter
Virginia, 1871

Two and one-fourth pounds of white sugar, two ounces of tartaric acid, juice of one lemon and three pints of water; boil together five minutes; when nearly cold, add the whites of three eggs beaten to a froth, half a cupful of flour well beaten with the egg and half an ounce of wintergreen essence or any other kind preferred; bottle, and keep in a cool place.

rotating rack holding several dozen dispenser bottles of sweetened, flavored syrups.

Some pharmacists used a vanilla syrup with a dollop of fresh cream to flavor their soda water; these "cream sodas" grew quickly in popularity. At an 1874 exposition in Philadelphia, one harried beverage vendor found himself out of fresh cream. He ran to a nearby confectionery and bought vanilla ice cream, planning to allow it to melt before using it. His impatient customers wouldn't wait, though, and thus was born another American favorite, the ice cream soda.

Probably the first bottled commercial soft drink in America was sold by French immigrant Eugene Roussel in Philadelphia. Roussel (who also ran a perfumery) laced his soda water with lemon flavor before bottling it for sale locally. He also shipped his lemon sodas to New York City. Now a number of new terms entered the American vocabulary. "Soda," for example, derived from soda water, an inaccurate name for water carbonated by artificial means (it didn't really contain soda). "Pop," a nickname for soft drinks, came from the sound of a cork being withdrawn from a bottle of root beer. "Pop" has been a part of the American vocabulary since about 1830.

From Corks to Caps

The invention of the modern "crown," or crimped metal, bottle cap revolutionized the American beverage industry. Patented in 1892, the crown cap enabled the quick and easy sealing of 100 bottles or more per minute. This was a lot faster than the hand process of inserting corks and tying them down with wire or string! While there had been alternatives to corks, they all involved expensive bottles. One type included a glass ball that was held by pressure against a gasket at the top of the bottle. Another type was the bail-top bottle, still in occasional use today; this bottle seems to have entered the market about 1875. The bail-top bottle featured a piece of metal, much like a bucket bail, which held down a porcelain cap and rubber gasket. A real advantage of the crown cap was that the bottles could be plain and inexpensive.

By the late 1800s, bottled soft drinks were becoming quite common. Americans no longer had to go to a soda fountain to get a soda. The most popular flavor was not the lemon soda pioneered by Roussel but, rather, the familiar ginger ale. Americans already knew the fermented version, which had been made on farms for generations. The fermented beverage was called ginger beer; the new soft drink was almost always labeled ginger ale. Another early soft drink was root beer, again quite familiar to rural and small-town Americans. Philadelphia druggist Charles Hires went a long way toward popularizing root beer among urbanites who had never seen a sassafras tree. His fountain beverage attracted a lot of notice at the 1876 Centennial exposition. In Waco, Texas, pharmacist Wade Morrison in 1885 pushed a concoction he called Dr Pepper, named after a colleague back east who had driven Morrison off for romancing Pepper's daughter. In Toronto, residents were treated to Canada Dry Ginger Ale, a beverage so successful that it was soon marketed in the United States.

The only thing that remained was to make soft drinks as American as beer. Coca-Cola, with its extracts of coca leaf and cola nut, was the fastest-growing soft drink in the United States in the twentieth century. It began in the vats of an Atlanta physician named John S. Pemberton, who prescribed it for headache and hangover. In 1894, Joseph A. Biedenharn first put Coca-Cola into bottles, for the refreshment of plantation workers near Vicksburg, Mississippi. By the first years of the new century, Coca-Cola was in the midst of a gargantuan advertising campaign, urging Americans to take that "Pause That Refreshes." The Dr Pepper Company was no more aggressive than the others when it urged customers to drink a Dr Pepper "at ten, two, and four."

The Legacy of Prohibition

It is possible that the art of making traditional brewed root beers would have died out, or nearly so, if not for the advent of that social experiment called Prohibition. In an attempt to curb the excesses of American drinking (which admittedly added up to an average annual consumption of around 3 gallons of grain alcohol for every man, woman, and child), Congress made it a crime to "make, sell, or transport" alcoholic beverages. This led to a strong citizen interest in the illegal hobby of homebrewing, and a vast number of American families laid in supplies of bottles and bottle caps, and purchased cast-iron bottle cappers. With all that investment it paid to get the most out of these purchases. If Grandpa or Grandma were making homebrew

Root Beer

Recipe of Mrs. Lida Seely
United States, 1902

This wholesome drink, which was made every spring in the households of our American forebears, is delicious as well as healthful, and it is a pity that the use of genuine root beer is dying out. The sarsaparilla, yellow dock, dandelion, burdock, and hops used for its making were all products of the nearby woods and fields. Bark of the wild cherry was sometimes put in, birch bark also, and elecampane, and the aromatic spikenard. In springtime children went out with trowel and basket, and their intimate knowledge of the growths about them helped to their brewing.

The roots should be all thoroughly washed and then bruised. To two gallons of water take an ounce each of the ingredients. Put the roots in the cold water and set them over the fire so that the heating will draw all the essences and flavors of the growths. Let them steep about half an hour and then strain. Add a pound of sugar and about twenty-five drops of the oil of sassafras or spruce, and, when the brew is cool enough not to kill the yeast, add say six or eight tablespoons to the above quantity of water, or a dry yeast-cake or two dissolved in a little tepid water. Stir the yeast in well and set the brew away in an earthen jar and give it some hours to work. After three or four hours it may be bottled or kept in the jar for immediate drinking without bottling.

beer, why shouldn't Mom make an occasional batch of root beer? Yeast companies capitalized on the new interests of so many Americans, and circulated recipes for old-fashioned root beers. Those who preferred a faster and simpler product could take advantage of the brand name bottled extracts sold by Hires, McCormick's, and other companies.

Prohibition came to an end in 1933. President Franklin D. Roosevelt sought to create jobs in Milwaukee, St. Louis, and many other cities, and needed to find a new product to tax. The bottles and bottle cappers were moved into the cellars, and most American families forgot about homebrewed beers and soft drinks.

Renewed Interest in Self-Sufficiency

By the mid-1960s, young people in particular began to reject the everywhere-the-same aspect of American life, that cultural homogenization brought about by consumers all using identical factory-made goods. These young people studied the arts of weaving, dying, leatherwork, and candle making. At the same time, they developed an interest in foods and drinks that were made from scratch. A flood of recipe books from the period emphasized the joys of homemade breads, homegrown vegetables, home-sprouted sprouts, and home-brewed teas, ciders, and bottled drinks.

Some writers nowadays poke fun at the naïveté of the youthful counterculture, and at some of the internal contradictions of its rebellion against America's industrial society. But there is a lot to be said for knowing how to do things for yourself and not relying on corporations for every item of your food, clothing, and shelter. Making things from scratch helps you appreciate the things you have and spurs you to use your creativity.

If you are like me, you have found that American soft drinks are so incredibly sweet as to be almost undrinkable. I believe it is much better for each of us to tailor our own recipes to our own tastes. Gathering wild plants to use as ingredients keeps us in tune with nature and provides sunshine, exercise, fun, and fresh air. The whole family can participate in foraging expeditions and in the afternoons spent around a pot of simmering root beer.

Equipment

hen I first started to make beverages at home, I read several books, carefully selected and bought every recommended piece of equipment, and rigorously sanitized each piece before use. My friend Mike Tawes, however, provided a different example.

Feeding his interest in wine making, Mike rinsed out a half-gallon apple juice jar, then filled it with dandelion flowers, water, and sugar. After a few days he screwed on the lid. Every now and then he unscrewed the lid to let the carbon dioxide whoosh out, as the natural yeast from the flowers and the air fermented the sugary mixture. Twelve months later it was tasty wine!

The point is, you can have success using either store-bought equipment or improvised gear. Those who are sure they will be making many batches of beverages may very well want to purchase additional items to save time and effort. My aim, though, is to allow the reader to make small batches with few or no purchases of equipment.

Basic Equipment

While purist homebrewers may cringe at the very short list of equipment I claim is necessary, any reasonably appointed kitchen already contains most of the items you'll need for making soft drinks and, for that matter, beers. Additional items are chiefly labor-saving devices.

Bottle capper. Bottle cappers come in a variety of styles and range in price from a couple of dollars for a primitive design to twenty times as much for a nice table model.

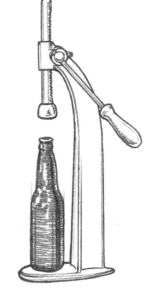

Bottle cappers range from cheap models that use a hammer to provide the pressure, to nice table models made of plastic or steel. This model came from a farm auction and has a lot of personality. The seller insisted that her husband had used it only for the making of *root* beer.

This affordable stockpot has all the basic requirements of a brewpot: construction of medium-gauge stainless steel, a capacity of 3 gallons, and two handles for stable lifting. But even a pot with a capacity of only 2 quarts will allow you to get started making root beers.

Brewpot. This should be made of stainless steel, glass, or enameled steel. A 6-quart pot is advisable, but a 1-gallon pot will work, too. Most well-equipped kitchens may already have a pot you can use. If you don't own a pot matching the brewpot's description, a small enamel canner will be the most cost-efficient purchase. A pot of 3 to 4 gallons will allow the efficient making of larger batches, up to 5 gallons. For 5-gallon batches of truly excellent beverages, a 6-gallon pot is recommended. Still, I encourage the beginner to use a pot that is on hand or to purchase a small canner.

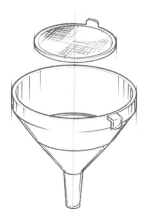

This funnel meets all the requirements of the home beverage maker: It is made of food-grade plastic, has a large capacity (about 1 quart), is heat resistant, and comes with a snap-in strainer that allows you to pour and strain with only two hands and minimal mess.

Funnels. Two funnels, one large and one small, will come in handy to transfer liquids from container to container. The preferred material here is stainless steel or heat-resistant food-grade plastic. It is useful to have a strainer built into the larger funnel. Homebrew suppliers sell a funnel with a built-in strainer that pops out for cleaning. Or you may be able to improvise a strainer using a thin layer of cheesecloth.

Jug or carboy. The bare necessity for a novice brewer is a 1-gallon container made of glass or food-grade plastic. A milk jug will work in a pinch, but I recommend a glass jug of the sort that apple cider comes in. Those who go on to make larger batches should probably invest in a glass carboy; this is simply a very large, squat bottle made of thick glass. Most homebrewers buy the 5-gallon size,

The glass carboy is the vessel traditionally used by beverage makers. These are readily available in sizes ranging from 3 to 7 gallons. Makers of small batches of beverage may substitute a couple of 1-gallon glass cider jugs.

although for the more ambitious, 6- and 7-gallon carboys are readily available. For the less ambitious, a 3-gallon size is fine.

Brewers of large batches of drink will find that the carboy is not an especially formidable expense, but those who wish to save money may want to find instead a 5- or 6-gallon pail made of food-grade plastic. These are often available from restaurants, bakeries, and doughnut shops. Like the carboys, they are also available from homebrew suppliers (see Appendix A). The pail should have a lid. Keep an eye out for these food-grade plastic pails, as it may eventually prove helpful to own several of them. Do not use plastic buckets that once held paint, putty, asphalt, or anything else potentially toxic. These buckets are not of food-grade quality and are impossible to clean properly.

If clean bottles are soaked in a solution of water with a small amount of chlorine bleach, there is little danger of the beverage becoming "infected" with microorganisms that produce off-flavors. The typical 5-gallon plastic pail will hold thirteen bottles in a single layer.

Sanitizing pail. For soaking bottles before filling, you'll need a bucket or clean plastic trash pail. The 5-gallon food-grade plastic pails described above will hold about thirteen bottles standing upright in a single layer. If you have a large collection of bottles you may want to use a 10- or 15-gallon trash pail.

Thermometer. A thermometer for measuring the temperature of the liquids you are working with is on almost everybody's list of essential brewing equipment. The best kind is at least 8 inches long, and will go as low as 32°F and as high as 212°F. A thermometer is a very useful piece of equipment, especially for telling you when the temperature is appropriate for adding ("pitching") the yeast. If you would like to make just a few batches of drink without purchasing a lot of equipment, however, you can get by for quite a while without a thermometer. The most important measure of temperature in these recipes is to determine when a liquid is lukewarm. Checking the temperature of the wort can be done with a finger; the potential problem is contamination of your beverage with microorganisms that can contribute off-flavors to the finished product. As much as your hands will be in and out of sanitizing solution on brewing day, though, a good wash and rinse in very hot water should allow you safely to put a finger into the warm liquid. Use just your knuckle; it's sensitive enough to know when a liquid is lukewarm. Avoid immersing the fingernail, as sanitizing under the nail is almost impossible. I encourage you to buy a thermometer early in your brewing career, but I also attest from experience that you can make some excellent root beers without one.

Other essentials. The other items you will need for making beverages are things that any well-equipped kitchen already has: measuring cups, measuring spoons, and a large spoon for stirring.

A glass thermometer is not a necessity but will prove useful in deciding when it is time to "pitch" the yeast.

Bottles and Caps

Home beverage makers will need a supply of heavy glass bottles (non–screw top). Eleven 12-ounce bottles is the minimum, which will allow you to make and bottle 1 gallon of beverage. If you plan to make batches of 5 gallons, you will need fifty-three bottles. To go along with the bottles, you'll also need a supply of bottle caps. These are sold by the gross and are very inexpensive.

As your friends and relatives learn that you are starting to brew your own beverages, they are sure to regale you with tales of Grandpa or Grandma's exploding bottles. In years gone by, innumerable households were startled by the sound of exploding bottles and a heavy, sweet smell of yeasty beverages running across the floor. This book will explain several ways to prevent those exploding bottles.

HEAVY, UNTHREADED GLASS BOTTLES

One way to prevent such explosions is to use only strong, heavy bottles. Three beer brands that use such bottles are Samuel Adams, Beck's, and St. Pauli Girl. If you're lucky, you may find returnable bottles made of heavy glass. An overnight soak in warm water with a little household ammonia will suffice to get the paper labels off. *Note:* For safety's sake, never allow an ammonia solution to come in contact with a solution containing chlorine bleach or any other chemicals.

BAIL-TOP BOTTLES

Another solution to curb the threat of exploding bottles is to lay in a supply of 16-ounce bail-top beer bottles. These bottles are nice because of their classic design, which does not require the use of bottle caps. A lever action and a rubber gasket will keep the carbonation in. These bottles are not always easy to find, but a store with a good selection of beer will have one or more brands using bail-top bottles (such as Grolsch and Altenmünster).

A variety of bottles will work for homemade beverages, including bail-top bottles, high-quality beer bottles, and old returnable soft drink bottles.

The Demise of Good-Quality Glass Bottles

I am sorry to report that fewer and fewer beverage manufacturers are using high-quality bottles. As each year passes, breweries prove more willing to use light, thin-walled glass bottles. The elegant porcelain tops of the bail-top bottles are giving way to plastic tops. Soft-drink makers eschew glass bottles and instead use very thin plastic bottles with an insert at the bottom that makes the bottle's capacity seem larger than it is. Do what you can to locate high-quality glass bottles. Sheer weight is a good, though not infallible, indication of a bottle's strength. Imported beers tend to come in stronger bottles than do American beers, but this is not a hard-and-fast rule. Seek out unthreaded bottles, because typically their broader lip means a superior seal. *Note:* You want bottles without threads, but some unthreaded bottles are thin-walled and weak while others are heavy and strong.

BUILDING YOUR BOTTLE SUPPLY

As you begin to brew larger batches of beverages and to have a stock of several beverages on hand at once, it will eventually prove necessary to own four or five dozen or even more high-quality bottles. Fortunately, this stockpile may be built up gradually. Beer-drinking friends are a good source. Recycling groups may consent to give you appropriate bottles, since refilling old bottles is a more ecologically sound practice than remanufacturing them into a new glass product. Larger homebrew supply stores and mail-order houses have new bottles for sale, but the price is just high enough that you will find that for only a few cents more per bottle you can buy them with a beverage inside! Flea markets and even old rural trash dumps can be a good source for old soda bottles, often with interesting designs, logos, and slogans on them. Needless to say, a great deal of cleaning and sanitizing may be in order, but these bottles do have a certain charm, and the price is usually right. The older bottles often have the advantage of being smaller — sometimes holding just 6 or 7 ounces. These small bottles are useful for testing the carbonation to see if a batch of soft drink is ready. You may also find that you do not always want to drink a full 12-ounce soft drink. (I can't help but bemoan a remarkable change: We have gone from being a nation where 6 ounces of soft drink was a pleasant treat, to being a land of convenience stores selling 32-ounce paper cups of soft drink to be consumed at one sitting!)

A WORD OF CAUTION

Unless you have an excellent source of good bottles — a mole in a local pub, for example — or already have enough of them, you may begin to wonder if it is really so necessary to use heavy, glass, unthreaded bottles. Will threaded bottles work? What about plastic soda bottles? The short answer is that both of these kinds of bottles will work to create the beverage. This is an example of how conventional wisdom changes. Ten years ago, all guides to homebrewing insisted that heavy, glass, unthreaded bottles were essential for carbonated beverages such as beer. After a time, though, people came forward who said, "I always use threaded disposable bottles, and I've never had any trouble." So yes, threaded bottles can be used. There is a special type of bottle cap designed for threaded bottles, but even regular caps can give good results.

Still, I want to inject a note of caution. Heavy, unthreaded bottles offer the best protection against explosions. Although homebrewers do not often experience them, most have experienced an explosion at least once. This unwelcome event is more likely to occur when using thin bottles of the threaded variety. This point is more important for makers of soft drinks than for brewers of beer. Considering how volatile the mixture of bulk sugar with water and yeast is in a closed container, the home soft-drink maker is urged to choose bottles carefully. Unless you are desperate for bottles and are willing to run the risk of a big mess and loss of beverage, stick to the heavy glass bottles when making soft drinks.

Plastic soda bottles both large and small will also work for making beers and soft drinks. The chief potential problem here is the cap, which uses threads plus a squishy plastic liner to make a seal. The cap may be reusable four times or eight times, but eventually it will fail. The trick is predicting when the cap is ready to be discarded. Part of the equation is, how many times has the bottle been resealed after drinking only part of the contents? I prefer heavy glass bottles to plastic because the glass bottles are more ecologically sound. Glass is made of abundant materials such as sand; plastic is made from relatively scarce petroleum products. Glass can be reused countless times without modification; plastic bottles have a limited number of uses and then must either be remanufactured or buried. Still, if you do get into a bind for bottles, be aware that plastic soda bottles will work, usually with good results.

 Long-Necked Bottles

Ever wonder why bottles are shaped the way they are, with wide shoulders and a narrow neck? The answer is that this design allows you to pour a beverage without getting the sediment into the glass. Hold the bottle up to the light the first time you pour a homemade root beer, and you can see what's happening. (You'll find it easiest to see into a clear or green bottle.) The sediment will gradually make its way to the shoulder but won't go into the glass if you are careful. To avoid a strong yeast taste, pour your homemade beverages slowly, leaving about half an inch in the bottle, and most of the yeast will stay in the bottle — together with any stray bits of bark or twig. The yeast taste is less strong starting about two days after the bottles are moved to the refrigerator. Use of ale yeast instead of bread yeast will result in a beverage in which most of the yeast has settled out and thus won't be tasted. If you relish the taste of yeast, simply drink from the bottle and don't worry about it!

Nonessential but Helpful Items

While any other equipment won't improve the flavor of soft drinks, some extras can certainly make beverage making easier.

Bottle brush. A good bottle brush is a nice thing to have. Your brush should be long enough to reach the bottom of any bottle.

Scale. A postal scale can take away some of the guesswork when gauging the weight of ingredients.

Siphon tubing. If you plan to make large batches, you'll want to purchase additional equipment for transferring liquids. A piece of tubing made out of food-grade plastic, ⅜-inch inside diameter and about 3 feet long, will allow you to siphon liquids from one container to the other. This hose is a real help in making 5-gallon batches of drink.

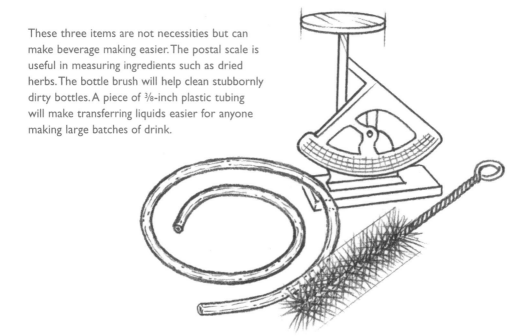

These three items are not necessities but can make beverage making easier. The postal scale is useful in measuring ingredients such as dried herbs. The bottle brush will help clean stubbornly dirty bottles. A piece of ⅜-inch plastic tubing will make transferring liquids easier for anyone making large batches of drink.

Basic Equipment

Bottle capper and bottle caps (not needed if using
   bail-top bottles)

Brewpot

Funnels, large and small

Glass bottles, unthreaded, heavy

Jug, carboy, or food-grade plastic pail

Kitchen spoon, large

Measuring cups and spoons

Pail for soaking bottles and other items in sanitizing
   solution (a food-grade plastic pail can serve double-
   duty, as both a soaking pail and a fermenter)

Nonessential but Nice

Bottle brush

Postal scale

Siphon tube, ⅜-inch inside diameter (useful for making
   large batches)

Thermometer

Equipment for the Experienced Brewer

After making a number of batches of bottled beverages, you may
be wondering what pieces of equipment, and what new procedures, could improve the quality of your beverages or simplify
the process of making them. Only after making a few gallons of
drink can you really know if you would like to invest in more
tools, vessels, and devices. It is easiest to learn to make beverages
using simple equipment; then, gradually, you can add the various
complications.

What follows is a discussion of additions to the basic equipment
collection of brewpot, jug or carboy, and rubber hose that will make
beverage making easier.

The bottling bucket allows for easy transfer of the soft drink to the bottles using a plastic hose. After you have mixed the ingredients and added the yeast, fit the plastic hose to the spigot and use the hose to fill the bottle. (This latter task can be further simplified by buying a filler tube.) Because the spigot is located an inch or so above the bottom of the fermenter, the dregs will be conveniently left behind. Bottling buckets are especially useful for batches of 2 gallons or more of drink.

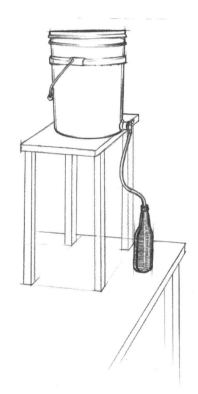

Bottling bucket. This bucket is really a 5-gallon pail made of food-grade plastic. These can be purchased from homebrew suppliers, or may be salvaged from restaurants or doughnut shops, where they once contained mayonnaise or vanilla crème. The purchased fermenters will have a little spigot near the bottom. If you are reusing a pail from a restaurant, buy just the spigot from a homebrew supplier, and attach it yourself after drilling a suitable hole.

The filler tube is an item that will greatly simplify the transferring of liquids from one container to another.

This glorified bucket can be useful in two ways. In making large batches it provides a good mixing container, and if the recipe calls for a couple of hours of fermenting prior to bottling (as with many citrus drinks), this early fermentation can take place in the bucket. The plastic bottling bucket is cheaper than a carboy, and easier to clean since you can reach down into it.

Filler tube. This is an inexpensive piece of equipment that can greatly simplify your life if you are bottling batches of 2 gallons or more of drink. The filler tube is simply a rigid plastic tube fitted with a valve and trigger on one end. Attach one end of your plastic hose to the spigot on your bottling bucket and the other end to this filler tube. When the trigger contacts the bottom of the bottle, the bottle begins to fill with beverage. When the bottle is full to the brim, pull up on the rigid tube. The trigger will release, and the flow stops. The filler tube displaces an amount of liquid just equal to the "headspace" of air you want to leave in the bottle. Thus, if you lift up on the filler tube just as the liquid reaches the bottle's rim, the quantity of drink in each bottle will be just right.

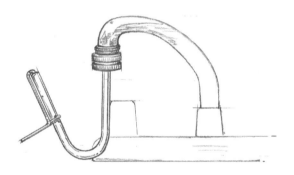

The jet-spray bottle washer screws onto the kitchen faucet. This one is now ready to clean the first bottle.

Put the bottle over the spindle of the jet-spray washer. When the bottle comes in contact with the trigger, water shoots into the bottle at a high rate of speed.

Jet-spray bottle washer. This inexpensive little brass device is a godsend when you're trying to maintain a collection of fifty or more reasonably clean glass bottles. The device screws onto the faucet of a standard laundry sink, or (with an adapter) onto the faucet of any kitchen sink. It has a built-in trigger device, such that when a bottle is put on the spindle, a jet of water rushes up into it, thoroughly cleansing it of traces of yeast and other sediments. This is not a substitute for rinsing containers immediately after use, but it is a big help after soaking and just before bottling. It is also useful for cleaning newly acquired bottles that may have anything from cigarette ashes and mouse droppings to dried cola in them. As a bonus, the jet-spray bottle washer also works well with jugs and carboys.

The jet-spray bottle washer and other items in this section are available from homebrew and wine-making suppliers (see Appendix A).

Racking tube. The racking tube is a big help when you want to brew 4- or 5-gallon batches of soft drink. It is simply a rigid tube that attaches to the plastic hose you use when siphoning liquids out of the carboy. The tube's prominent bend directs the siphoned liquid downward toward its destination (the bottles, or a large container). While your flexible plastic hose can also bend to direct the flow downward, the hose may kink, and the flow will slow or even stop. This often happens subtly, and you may waste some time before you discover that the flow has slowed substantially. While the racking tube is one more thing to purchase and one more item to sanitize, the price is very low and it does make transferring liquids a little quicker and easier. If you plan to make regularly 4- and 5-gallon batches of beverage, the racking tube is a wise purchase.

Spare refrigerator. This may not be as major an investment as it seems at first glance. You can probably benefit from someone's tired old cast-off refrigerator, discarded because the door is badly chipped, or because the freezer "doesn't keep ice cream anymore." In fact, the more important cost may not be the yard-sale price, but the cost of running a second refrigerator as seen on your monthly electric bill. Still, if you are serious about making beverages, the cost of a used refrigerator and the energy it takes to run it will prove worthwhile in the long run.

For makers of soft drinks, a spare refrigerator can be invaluable. Now you can enjoy the efficiency of making 4 or 5 gallons of beverage at a time and still feel confident that you will not be hearing the sickening crash of an exploding bottle or seeing the impressive white "gusher" of an overactive root beer. Making 5-gallon batches and storing them in this extra refrigerator will substantially decrease your time investment in beverage making. Storage here does have its limits, though, depending on such factors as the refrigerator's temperature and the kind and quality of your yeast. In most cases, storage of six to eight weeks or more will be possible.

If you need extra room for storing beverages but balk at the cost and space requirements of the full-size appliance, a "dormitory-size" refrigerator may be the answer. These typically will hold only a gallon or two of bottled beverage, but that may be all you need. To get the best prices on small, used refrigerators, visit a college campus in May and read the bulletin boards. Dormitory refrigerators are often available at bargain prices as the school year ends and may be only one or two years old.

Preventing Burnout

After an initial rush of enthusiasm, you may find yourself making fewer batches of beverage. While family members are begging for more of your famous raspberry-anise soda, you may dread going through the process. First you'll need to clean the kitchen to get your work area ready. Then you'll need to sanitize all your equipment. Now you can begin the brewing, cooling, pitching the yeast, bottling, and capping. Depending on how dirty your kitchen was to start with, and how complex your soft drink recipe, you may find yourself investing 2 hours in the making of eleven bottles of soda. Considering all of this, your brain may convince your heart that the payoff is not worth the time you've devoted.

MAKE LARGER BATCHES

Clearly, one way to come up with more bottles of soda for each hour of work is to make larger batches. If you have a big picnic or family reunion coming up, you may well want to make a 5-gallon batch of drink, timing it carefully to have it on ice in coolers, ready to drink when the guests arrive. If you're lucky, you may have a dozen or so soft drinks left over after the partygoers have gone home. As I mentioned earlier, if you acquire an extra refrigerator (or if you have an extra-chilly root cellar or basement that is always above freezing), you can routinely make larger batches and not have to worry about overcarbonation. While it is true that making a 5-gallon batch takes longer than making a 1-gallon batch, you will get more bottles per hour when you make larger batches. Presumably you can also brew drinks less often if you make larger batches, and burnout will be less likely.

Use Larger Bottles

One way to make your beverage-making days go more smoothly is to bottle your drink in quart or liter bottles. The plastic quart bottles were discussed earlier (see page 18); heavy glass quart bottles are also available. Several beer companies market quarts or liters in unthreaded bottles; flea markets often have old quart soda bottles made of heavy glass. Many champagne bottles, though not all, will accept a standard bottle cap. As a last resort, homebrew suppliers sell new quart bottles. The advantage of using quart or liter bottles is clear: fewer bottles to clean, sanitize, fill, cap, and store. Wow! A 1-gallon batch will take only four bottles. A 5-gallon batch of beverage will fit in twenty bottles instead of fifty-three. The time savings will be substantial. The only drawback is a certain loss of flexibility. What if you want to consume a single glass of drink and you can't find someone to share with you? Chances are that by the time you are ready for a second drink, some or all of the carbonation will have departed. Still, bottling in quart bottles will be a wise choice for many.

Keg Your Beverage

Another way to save considerable time on brewing day is to invest in a kegging system. Doing so can eliminate the work of constantly maintaining a bottle collection. After brewing, put your several gallons of beverage into the stainless-steel keg. The soft drink will be dispensed by the pressure of carbon-dioxide gas you inject into the keg.

The most popular type of kegging system for soft drinks is the Cornelius keg. If you have ever worked in a restaurant you are already familiar with these tall silver canisters with hoses attached, which are commonly used to store and serve commercial soft drinks. Many homebrewers use these same kegs to dispense their beer, rejoicing at their liberation from the need to bottle their grog. Cornelius kegs are readily available in 2½- and 5-gallon sizes, among others. You might be able to make room in the family refrigerator for a 2½-gallon Cornelius keg, while you could make a home for two or more of the 5-gallon size in your spare.

Another system, relatively new to the homebrewing world — and it works for soft drinks as well as beer — is the "party keg," a small plastic keg that holds about 5 liters, or just over 1 U.S. gallon. The price of a used Cornelius system is a little more than that for a new party keg system, when you factor in the "extras" such as taps, carbon-dioxide cartridges, and pressure pouches. The Cornelius system is extremely durable and will undoubtedly outlive the party keg. On the other hand, the party keg leaves a very small footprint in your refrigerator, and that may be a plus for you.

Now for the negatives. My prejudice against kegging systems is perhaps a silly one: I enjoy the historical angle of making traditional beverages, and part of that is using bottle caps and bail-top bottles. I prefer the historical process of fermentation to the artificial introduction of carbon dioxide. Other disadvantages of kegging systems are the initial high cost and the "upkeep" cost, including the price of carbon-dioxide cartridges. Nor do kegging systems free you from the necessity of sanitizing, since you must sanitize the keg itself as well as all hoses, connections, and fittings. Also, if you keg your beverage, it is no longer such an easy matter to take a sample over to a friend's house. But to end on a positive note, the kegging system will simplify your life considerably on brewing day, and will allow you to stop storing and maintaining your collection of dozens or even hundreds of bottles. By using carbon-dioxide injection, you should be able to store your soft drinks much longer than you can with bottled drinks. And finally, if you want to avoid even tiny amounts of alcohol, you may rest assured that drinks carbonated by carbon-dioxide injection contain no alcohol at all. (Be sure to drop yeast from the recipe when using kegging systems, because use of carbon-dioxide gas *replaces* the natural fermentation.)

The 5-liter plastic "party keg" is an inexpensive, time-saving alternative to bottling.

chapter 3

First Batches:
Root Beer and
Ginger Ale

This book contains dozens of recipes for root beer, birch beer, fizzes, sodas, coolers, ginger ale, and other drinks, including some that are taken from the pages of history. To start, though, you should try some simple recipes. What follows is a detailed run-through of the process of making a basic ginger ale and a basic root beer.

The Importance of Good Sanitation

Failures caused by lack of proper sanitation are a serious matter. While it is true that homemade beverages are not a source of botulism or other poisons, microscopic intruders *can* give a variety of off-tastes to fresh-made drinks, ranging from sour to cabbagelike. After brewing a bad batch, the home beverage maker must take steps to eradicate the tiny foes, or bad batches will occur with depressing regularity.

Develop standard procedures that keep your equipment clean and sanitary. Don't drive yourself crazy, of course, and don't take the fun out of beverage making: Just use common sense. Rinse *everything* in hot water immediately after use. It is much easier to clean a jug, carboy, pot, or spoon while it is still wet with ginger ale, than after it has dried and crusted for several hours. This goes for bottles, too — immediately after finishing a beverage, rinse the bottle with hot water and fill it to sit overnight before rinsing again. Then put it in your soaking pail filled with water and a little bleach. The bottles can remain in the soaking pail until their next use or can be rinsed and put away after a 2-hour soak. If you follow these procedures religiously, your bottles should seldom if ever need scrubbing or washing with detergent.

Before each brew session, soak all the utensils you intend to use in the bleach water, letting them sit for 30 minutes or longer. Among the items to be soaked are spoons, strainers, funnels, plastic hose, and the thermometer. Fill your jug or carboy with hot water and a little bleach and let it soak too. When you are ready to use a particular item, first rinse it in hot tap water.

 Sanitizing Styles

Each of us has to make his or her own choice about how much devotion sanitizing warrants. For some, the brewing area may approach laboratory standards; others may give each bottle a swish with very hot tap water and be done with it. I seem to err in the direction of "relaxed" brewing procedures, and I do experience bad batches on occasion. I suspect that those who are obsessed with sanitation have fewer failures.

SANITIZING BOTTLES

When you have gathered a supply of bottles, you will need to wash and sanitize them so they will be ready for the making of your first recipe. If the bottles seem reasonably clean, there should be no need to use any soap. Soap is rarely used in washing beverage bottles, but if you insist on it, soap must be very thoroughly rinsed out before the bottles are filled with drink. Hot water, soaking, and judicious use of a bottle brush will clean most bottles.

When your bottles are sparkling, fill your sanitizing pail with hot water to which you have added 2 tablespoons of unscented chlorine bleach per gallon. If possible, save the chlorine water, as it can sanitize more than a thousand clean bottles without needing to be changed. Ideally, you can dedicate one bucket to being your full-time bottle-sanitizing pail. *Caution:* Be especially careful while working with chlorine bleach; splashed drops of full-strength bleach will remove color from clothes, rugs, kitchen towels, and other materials and surfaces.

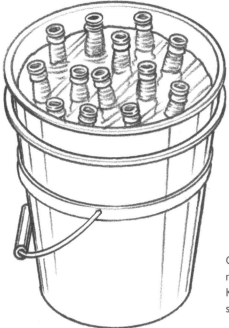

Check with restaurants, bakeries, and doughnut shops for 5-gallon food-grade plastic pails. Keep one filled with a chlorine solution for sanitizing bottles.

Making Root Beer

Root beer made from sassafras is the quintessential soft drink. Native Americans used sassafras root to make a tea and also used it to flavor a mixture of bear fat and crushed blackberries. English colonists in the 1600s made sassafras their major export, as Europeans sought the root as a cure for venereal disease. For mountaineers who settled in the Appalachians, sassafras tea was an important spring tonic, and root beer a tasty thirst quencher on a hot day. The recipe that follows is the simplest one in this book, in terms of ingredients, but it makes an incredibly good beverage.

$1/4$ ounce dried sassafras root bark
3 to 4 quarts water
2 cups sugar
$1/8$ teaspoon ale (or bread) yeast (also $1/4$ cup lukewarm water)

1. **Flavoring the water.** Place the pieces of root bark into a large pot. Add 2 quarts of the water and all the sugar. Simmer, covered, for 25 minutes. Still covered, remove from heat and let cool for another 25 minutes.

2. **Proofing the yeast.** Pour $1/4$ cup of lukewarm water into a teacup, then add the yeast. Let sit for several minutes.

3. **Straining into the jug.** Pour 1 quart cool water into the glass jug. Using a large funnel, slowly pour in the warm sassafras liquid, straining the liquid as you go.

4. **Adding water.** Aiming to make the overall temperature of the liquid in the jug lukewarm (70–76°F or 21–26°C), adjust the temperature of the remaining water and add it to the jug. Leave about 2 inches of headspace.

5. **Agitating.** Put the cap or a stopper on the jug and agitate vigorously for a few seconds.

6. **Adding yeast.** Remove the cap and add the yeast in its water. Cap again and shake the jug. Leave capped and let sit about 15 minutes.

7. **Topping off.** Finally, top off with warm water, cap loosely, and proceed immediately to bottling.

8. **Bottling.** Bottle according to the instructions in the box on page 34.

 Eleven 12-ounce bottles

Making Ginger Ale

Traditionally, ginger was not always used in the brewing process itself but was added later. American taverners sometimes kept an enormous shaker of fresh-ground ginger on the bar. The customer would shake in the ginger and the host would stir the drink with a red-hot poker. Those colorful days have passed, but ginger has not lost its popularity as a flavoring agent for beers and soft drinks. Savor the pleasant flavor of this gingery drink.

Ginger for Improved Taste

Medieval English brewers found it difficult to produce uniformly tasty beers. Their open crocks and vats were easily contaminated, and the result quite often was a beer that had an unpleasant off-taste. Brewers began casting about for the perfect ingredient to mask any unfortunate flavors. One of their favorite flavoring agents was ginger, an ingredient that seemed all the more mysterious and desirable because it came from "the East" via the legendary spice caravans.

1¼ ounces fresh gingerroot
3 to 4 quarts water
½ lemon, cut into several pieces
1¾ cups table sugar
⅛ teaspoon ale (or bread) yeast (also ¼ cup lukewarm water)

1. **Flavoring the water.** Grate the ginger coarsely into a large pot. Add 2 quarts of water, half the lemon, and the sugar. Simmer, covered, for 25 minutes. Still covered, remove from heat and let cool another 25 minutes.

2. **Proofing the yeast.** Pour ¼ cup of lukewarm water into a teacup, then add the yeast. Let sit for several minutes.

3. **Straining into the jug.** Pour 1 quart cool water into the glass jug. Using a large funnel, slowly pour in the warm ginger liquid, straining the liquid as you go.

4. **Adding water.** Aiming to make the overall temperature of the liquid in the jug lukewarm (70–76°F or 21–26°C), adjust the temperature of the remaining water and add it to the jug. Leave about 2 inches of headspace.

5. **Agitating.** Put the cap or a stopper on the jug and agitate vigorously for a few seconds.

6. **Adding yeast.** Remove the cap and add the yeast in its water. Cap again and shake the jug. Leave capped and let sit about 15 minutes.

7. **Topping off.** Finally, top off with warm water, cap loosely, and proceed immediately to bottling.

8. **Bottling.** Bottle according to the instructions in the box on page 34.

Eleven 12-ounce bottles

The step-by-step bottling instructions that follow are the same for all the modern soft drink recipes in this book. For a 1-gallon batch of drink, you will need eleven 12-ounce bottles and caps (or eight bail-top pint bottles with their reusable rubber gaskets).

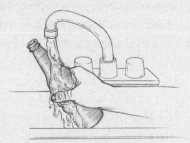

1. Remove your bottles from the sanitizing soak and rinse them well in very hot tap water.

2. Using the small funnel, fill each bottle from the jug.

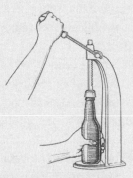

3. Using the bottle capper, cap the bottles.

4. Allow them to work (ideally at a room temperature of 62–77°F), checking after 48 hours and 72 hours. (During this period of "working," the yeast is consuming some of the sugar, and natural carbonation results from this process.) Carbonation time will depend on the quality of your yeast and the temperature of the room, among other factors. If the room is really hot, you may want to check after 36 hours.

5. When carbonation is right, put all bottles immediately into the refrigerator. For better flavor, wait a couple of days before drinking. The flavor improves after a few days because the yeast settles out, thus allowing your flavoring agents to shine through. Flavors also seem to improve by chemical processes I must admit I am unable to explain.

Why Bottles Explode

Farmers and farm wives of years gone by were well aware of the possibility of exploding bottles. Some recipes warned the maker to drink the beverage within a few days rather than let it sit in bottles as the carbonation continued to build. Some recipes were for a noncarbonated drink, to which the brewer could add a little baking soda in the glass to make the "fizz." Using modern methods of making alcoholic beers, exploding bottles are uncommon. Root beers and other soft drinks, however, are not as foolproof as beers when it comes to excessive carbonation.

Alcoholic beers do not explode, if properly made, because the yeast is allowed to consume all the sugars in the jug or carboy — and then the brewer notices that the fermentation has stopped, or nearly so. At bottling time, a small amount of sugar is added — to make the carbonation — but this amount is too little to allow the buildup of excessive carbonation. This process of adding sugar after fermentation has essentially ceased is called *priming* the beer.

In the making of soft drinks, however, we are just asking Mother Nature for trouble. We are bottling up yeast and a large amount of sugar and attempting to keep them under pressure. The traditional way of stopping the yeast's fermenting action was to move the bottles to a cool location, such as a root cellar or springhouse. (You could do what wine makers sometimes do and add chemicals to kill the yeast, but I prefer to avoid these additives.)

SLOWING YEAST ACTIVITY BY COOLING

My experience says that simply moving bottles to a cool location is often not enough to cause the yeast to cease its activity, especially if you want to store the drinks for more than a few days. At the least you may get a gusher when you open the bottle; at worst you will get an exploding bottle. One problem with gushing bottles is that a great deal of the beverage will end up on the floor or in the sink. Also, as the bottle gushes, the sediment (made up of yeast and bits of root) will rush up from the bottom and may end up in your drinking glass. Most people find homemade soft drinks taste better when the sediment remains on the bottom of the bottle.

FORMULA FOR SUCCESS

My game plan for preventing explosions and gushers is, first, always to use strong and heavy bottles. Second, I always put up a couple of very small bottles of root beer using old 6- or 7-ounce soft drink bottles that were popular in the 1940s and 1950s. I use these little bottles to test the root beer after 48 hours and again after 72 hours. (During the hot summertime, I make the first check after only 36 hours, since fermentation occurs more quickly at really warm temperatures.) If the root beer is dead — weak carbonation — I let the batch work some more. If the carbonation is just right, I immediately put all the bottles in the refrigerator and leave them there. Quickly moving the beverage to the refrigerator has two advantages: (1) The yeast begins to go dormant and the carbonation process almost ceases; and (2) chilled beverages are less likely to gush than are beverages at room temperature.

Admittedly, the disadvantage of my strategy is a crowded refrigerator. That's why I never make 5-gallon batches of root beer, unless they're for an event at which all the beverage will be consumed in short order. With the old-fashioned method, I several times experienced gushing beverages and broken bottles, especially after the root beers had sat for a couple of weeks. Since adopting the "refrigerator method," I have not suffered any such disappointments.

There are limits to refrigerator storage, of course. I said earlier that the carbonation process *almost ceases* with refrigerator storage. Unless your refrigerator is quite a bit colder than mine, you will probably find that carbonation does continue to build, though at a much reduced rate. After about five weeks, the bottles may begin to gush a bit when you open them. On the other hand, it is very rare for my wife and me to take five weeks to drink a gallon of root beer. If you find that a batch of soft drink is still in your refrigerator after five weeks, it is probably not a very tempting beverage, and you should decide whether to drink it now or discard it. (The precise storage life of your soft drinks will depend on the temperature of your refrigerator, the quality of the yeast you used, and the degree of carbonation present when the drinks were first chilled.)

The following chapters contain the recipes. Chapter 4 features some modern recipes for typical soft drinks including sarsaparilla soda, birch beer, and lemon-lime soda. Chapter 5 features harvest drinks, mulled beverages, and drinks that feature vinegar. Chapters 6 and 7 encourage you to devise your own recipes and offer some guidance on the use of various ingredients.

Now, on to the recipes!

Basic Modern Recipes

This chapter offers basic recipes for the most popular kinds of traditional soft drinks, including root beer, ginger ale, birch beer, and cream soda. You'll also find some newer concoctions, such as Chinese Ginger Beer and Maraschino Fizz. In all cases you are encouraged to use these recipes as a starting point and later to develop your own favorite recipes. Some people like ginger ale with a severe ginger "bite"; others prefer a milder drink. Some enjoy a very sweet root beer; others prefer less sugar and a more fierce carbonation. Whatever your preferences, you will be developing the expertise necessary to tailor recipes to suit your tastes. (Chapters 6 and 7 offer additional guidance in devising your own recipes.)

Spruce Beer

*Recipe of Norma Roberts
Bristol, New Hampshire, 1939*

1 gallon boiling water
¾ teaspoon oil of spruce
¾ teaspoon oil of sassafras
2 cakes compressed yeast
¾ teaspoon oil of wintergreen
4 gallons cold water
3 pints molasses

Pour boiling water over oil of spruce, sassafras, and wintergreen. Add cold water, molasses and yeast cakes. Let stand 2 hours, bottle, let stand 48 hours before using. Place on ice before serving. Makes 25 quart bottles.

Using and Measuring Natural Ingredients

Many of these soft drink recipes call for roots, bark, leaves, twigs, flowers, and sap. Gathering this material in field, meadow, and forest can be a very enjoyable experience. If you choose to gather wild plants, be sure to obtain a couple of good field guides to trees and wildflowers, and a good illustrated guide to edible plants as well. (Several of these guides are listed in the suggested reading.) There *are* poisonous plants out there, and the last thing you want to do is to accidentally make a soft drink from nightshade! Chapter 7 features a discussion of the ethics of gathering wild materials — be sure to read it before gathering any appreciable quantity of native plants.

For city dwellers, and others who have no place to forage, many health food stores have shelves of glass jars containing natural ingredients such as sassafras root bark, juniper berries, and burdock root. These stores are also a good source for plant materials whose geographic range does not include your home region — sassafras root for residents of the western United States, for example.

QUANTITY QUANDARIES

Many of the natural ingredients in these recipes present certain problems when it comes to specifying quantity. In the case of sassafras root, for example, I usually specify the number of inches of root, the thickness of a pencil. But what if the root is 1-inch thick? Specifying weight would not necessarily help, since a host of other questions arise:

- Is the sassafras you are using root bark only, or does it include the less pungent white wood as well?
- Is the root fresh or dried?
- If dried, has it been in storage three months or three years?
- Is the root chopped or whole?
- Was the root dug in early spring or in the late summer?
- Was the plant in vigorous, young growth or stately old age?
- Was the root dug in a Michigan meadow or in a coastal swamp in South Carolina?

In short, general guidelines for quantities can be suggested, but you will also need to use your eyes, nose, and taste buds. An ingredient such as sassafras will add color, aroma, and flavor to the brew water.

You may need to add more root, or add more water, after looking, smelling, and tasting. Fortunately, the measurements of these plant ingredients are never critical, and both a large and a small piece of sassafras root can yield an excellent drink. Even ingredients such as orange peel can vary widely from source to source: Does the peel include the white of the rind, or is it the zest only? Is the peel fresh or dried, and if dried, how long ago was it dried? Again, using your nose and taste buds will help. The making of tasty drinks does not require absolutely precise measurements of the natural flavoring ingredients.

SASSAFRAS ROOT

Since sassafras root appears in several of the following recipes, it might be well to add a few words about this particular ingredient. Sassafras root has traditionally appeared in all American herbals. The tea made from its roots was considered a valuable spring tonic. Some years ago, scientists discovered that if laboratory rats were fed very large quantities of safrole (the active ingredient in sassafras), they were more likely to develop cancer than were rats in a control group. The Food and Drug Administration (FDA) decreed that no safrole or sassafras could appear in processed food products such as bottled root beer for the retail market. Sassafras may, however, be sold as a raw food product, and herb suppliers usually have little bags of sassafras root bark for sale for teas.

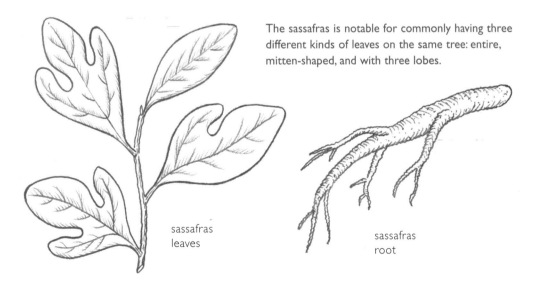

The sassafras is notable for commonly having three different kinds of leaves on the same tree: entire, mitten-shaped, and with three lobes.

sassafras
leaves

sassafras
root

The scientists' discoveries, predictably, created a storm of controversy that has yet to subside. Aficionados of herbs and alternative medicine doubt that a root that was valued for centuries as a tonic could be a significant carcinogen. They point out that humans, unlike the unfortunate laboratory rats, do not eat massive quantities of pure safrole — humans consume only very modest quantities of beverages made from sassafras root. My practice is to make several dozen bottles of root beer from sassafras root every year, and to avoid drinking more than one per day when I do have them on hand. I suspect that this is overcautious, but others may believe me reckless. If you prefer to avoid consumption of a beverage made from sassafras root, use bottled root beer extract instead. The extract contains artificial as well as natural flavors, of course, and many purists prefer to avoid all artificial flavoring.

Soft Drinks from Extracts

Extracts are worth mentioning as a quick and very inexpensive way to make soft drinks at home. The taste is usually very good, and the cost is about one-sixth that of a name brand soft drink. Despite the presence of artificial flavors (which in any case are present in store-bought beverages, too), the homemade product should be more healthful because you may include less sugar than is found in the national brands of soft drinks, and because the presence of yeast adds some B-complex vitamins.

There is no need to give recipes here for making soft drinks from extract. It is simply a matter of mixing extract, water, sugar, and yeast, according to the proportions given on the package, then bottling immediately. Two days later, the beverage is sufficiently carbonated to drink. You don't have to heat the ingredients when making soft drink from extract.

Most large grocery stores sell one or two brands of root beer extract, and they may sell one or two other beverage extracts as well. Look for these products on the shelf near the vanilla extract. Homebrew suppliers have a wider variety of soft drink extracts for sale. The flavors available include cola, ginger ale, root beer, birch beer, sarsaparilla, orange, grape, and cherry. While I prefer the fun — and the savings — of making soft drinks from scratch, when I'm in a hurry I find that the extracts fit the bill very well. You can, however, make your own root beer extract from the recipe on page 44.

During my 18-month career as a hand bookbinder, I discovered that making six copies of a blank journal at once was much more time-efficient than making six blank journals one at a time. So, too, with brewing and bottling root beers, the process can be made more efficient by making larger batches each time you brew. Yet you dare not make a 20-gallon batch, since storage of these volatile libations would present a problem. A better way to make larger batches is to produce your own extract, store it in canning jars at room temperature, then prepare gallons of soft drink as you need them. You'll save time without the worry of refrigerator storage space.

How Much to Make?

The soft drink recipes that follow make 1 gallon (eight 1-pint bottles or eleven 12-ounce bottles), unless otherwise noted. It is more efficient, in terms of number of bottles per hour of time invested, to make batches larger than 1 gallon. The problem with larger batches, mentioned earlier, is the possibility of gushing or even exploding bottles when they are allowed to sit too long at room temperature.

In deciding how much beverage to make, consider your family size, and how many friends and neighbors you expect to join you in trying out the finished product. How much soft drink do you plan to consume in the space of a week or ten days? How much storage space is available in your refrigerator? It may be that 2-, 3-, or even 5-gallon batches may be more appropriate for your needs. Simply multiply each ingredient in the recipe by the number of gallons you wish to make.

Homemade Root Beer Extract

This recipe allows you to make 8 gallons of root beer in extract form. You can then prepare 1-gallon batches as you need them simply by adding water and yeast to the extract and bottling. Making an extract more concentrated than the one described below would be possible, and would save space on your pantry shelf. Be constantly aware, however, of the dangers of scorching a highly concentrated sugary mixture. After trying this recipe, you may want to experiment with making extracts for other beverages. For this recipe, you need eight 1-quart canning jars with bands and lids. Ensure that canning jars, bands, and lids are cleaned and sanitized and that the rims of the jars are free of chips and cracks. Also, make sure you have a water bath or pressure canner that will hold eight 1-quart jars.

1½ cups raisins, coarsely chopped
3 cups boiling water
2 gallons water
1½ ounces dried sassafras root bark
7½ pounds (15 cups) sugar

1. Place raisins into a pan. Pour 3 cups boiling water over them and cover, allowing the raisins to steep.
2. Meanwhile, place 2 gallons water in the brewpot, over a medium heat, and add the sassafras root bark. As water heats, stir in the sugar slowly. Simmer, uncovered, for about 40 minutes.
3. Remove from heat and strain raisin water into the brewpot. Allow to sit, covered, for 30 minutes. You needn't worry about "wild yeast" infections; the canner will destroy any unwanted microbes.
4. Pour the extract into the canning jars. With a clean cloth, wipe off any spills on the rims. Put bands and lids in place and process in your canner. (Follow the instructions that came with your canner or with the bands and lids.)

Assuming all goes well and the dome lids seal properly, this extract can be stored almost indefinitely at room temperature.

 8 quarts of extract (makes 8 gallons of root beer)

Making Root Beer from Extract

1. To make up a 1-gallon batch of root beer, simply empty the contents of one of the quart jars into a pan containing 3 quarts of water. Heat gently to mix, but do not allow to get hotter than lukewarm.
2. Add ⅛ teaspoon ale yeast to the lukewarm liquid, bottle, and put the bottles in a dark place.
3. Check carbonation after 48 hours and again after 72 hours. When carbonation is right, refrigerate.

Hint

Getting all of the extract out of the jar is simple if you stand the jar in a large bowl of very hot water for 10 minutes or so before you begin.

Old-Fashioned Root Beer

Recipe of Fleischmann Yeast Company United States, 1912

1 cake, compressed yeast
5 pounds, sugar
2 ounces, sassafras root
1 ounce, hops or ginger root
2 ounces, juniper berries
4 gallons, water
1 ounce, dandelion root
2 ounces, wintergreen

Wash roots well in cold water. Add juniper berries (crushed) and hops. Pour 8 quarts boiling water over root mixture and boil slowly 20 minutes. Strain through flannel bag. Add sugar and remaining 8 quarts water. Allow to stand until lukewarm. Dissolve yeast in a little cool water. Add to root liquid. Stir well. Let settle and then strain again and bottle. Cork tightly. Keep in a warm room 5 to 6 hours, then store in a cool place. Put on ice as required for use.

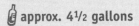 approx. 4½ gallons

Three-Root Root Beer

I took two different kinds of homemade beer and this root beer to a St. Patrick's Day party. I can't say that the homebrew made much of a stir, but the root beer got rave reviews and was gone in a matter of minutes. This is one of hundreds of variations of a traditional root beer recipe. The burdock is present largely as a traditional root beer ingredient with tonic qualities; the licorice root adds a subtle sweetness and flavor in this amount.

> 20 inches fresh-dug sassafras root, the thickness of a pencil
> 2 teaspoons chopped dried burdock root
> 2 teaspoons chopped dried licorice root
> 3 to 4 quarts water
> 1²/₃ cups table sugar
> ⅛ teaspoon ale yeast (also ¼ cup lukewarm water)

1. Place the roots in 2 quarts of water and simmer, uncovered, for about 25 minutes, adding the sugar toward the end. The water should take on a pronounced red or orange color, and the room should be filled with a strong sassafras aroma. If the color and aroma are weak, add more sassafras root. Remove from heat, cover, and let cool for 30 minutes.

2. Pour 1 quart of cool water into the jug or carboy. After the sassafras mixture has cooled 30 minutes, strain it slowly into the jug. Add water to the jug, leaving a headspace of 2 inches and aiming for an overall lukewarm temperature (70–76°F or 21–26°C). If the temperature is too high, allow the liquid to cool with the cap on; this cooling may take some time. With the cap on the jug, agitate vigorously.

3. In a teacup, combine the yeast and ¼ cup lukewarm water; let sit about 5 minutes. Add the yeast liquid to the jug, agitate, and then bottle the beverage.

4. After about 48 hours — sooner in warm rooms, later in cool rooms — check the carbonation. If it's sufficient, refrigerate the bottles.

 Eleven 12-ounce bottles

Rich Root Beer

When in Morgantown, West Virginia, my wife and I always visit a specialty store called A Slight Indulgence. One day we sampled an imported English root beer with a delightfully full-bodied flavor. The label bragged about such barely perceptible ingredients as anise and wintergreen, but it neglected to mention one especially rich ingredient that was right on the tips of our tongues (literally). Finally we realized what it was — vanilla.

While I did not aim to reproduce the English recipe, our visit to Morgantown inspired me to develop a recipe for a sinfully rich root beer so luxurious that it even includes a foamy head!

> 20 inches sassafras root, the thickness of a pencil
> 1 piece vanilla bean, 3 inches long
> 3 to 4 quarts water
> 1¾ cups dark brown sugar, gently packed
> ⅛ teaspoon ale yeast (also ¼ cup lukewarm water)

1. Place the root and vanilla bean in 2 quarts of water and simmer, uncovered, for about 25 minutes, adding the sugar toward the end. Water should take on a pronounced red or dark orange color, and the room should be filled with a strong sassafras aroma. If the color and aroma are weak, add more sassafras root. Remove from heat, cover, and let cool for 30 minutes.

2. Put 1 quart of cool water into the jug. After the sassafras mixture has cooled 30 minutes, pour it slowly into jug. Add water to the jug, leaving a headspace of about 2 inches and aiming for a lukewarm overall temperature. (If the temperature of the liquid is above lukewarm, allow it to cool.) Cap the jug and agitate vigorously.

3. In a teacup, combine the yeast and ¼ cup lukewarm water, and let sit about 5 minutes. Add the yeast liquid to the jug, agitate, and then bottle the beverage. After about 48 hours — sooner in warm rooms, later in cool rooms — check the carbonation; when sufficient, refrigerate.

 Eleven 12-ounce bottles

Licorice Root Beer

The well-known taste of black licorice candy really is a blend of three separate flavors: licorice, molasses, and anise. This soft drink uses all three to duplicate that favorite childhood flavor. Together they provide a very refreshing and pleasant beverage.

The Three Flavors of Licorice Candy

Licorice root is native to the Mediterranean region, and most of the roots found for sale today still come from that part of the world. Herbalists prescribe licorice for coughs and hoarseness, but the root is most commonly used as a flavoring and sweetener in candies and in beer.

Molasses is another source of flavor and sweetness.

Anise has been enjoyed for thousands of years. The ancient Romans used it as a cough suppressant, digestive aid, condiment, and antidote for poisons. It was such an important herb for the English that an early Virginia law required every colonist to bring and plant six anise seeds!

4 tablespoons chopped dried licorice root
3 tablespoons molasses
1½ cups sugar
2 teaspoons anise extract
4 quarts water
⅛ teaspoon granulated ale yeast
(also ¼ cup lukewarm water)

1. Place the licorice root, molasses, and sugar in 2 quarts of water and simmer, uncovered, for 10 minutes. Remove from heat, add the anise extract, and cover. Allow to steep for 30 minutes more. Pour the remaining 2 quarts of cool water into a 1-gallon glass jug, then strain in the contents of the brewpot.
2. Place the ale yeast into a teacup containing the ¼ cup of lukewarm water and allow to sit for several minutes.
3. After verifying that the contents of the jug are not hotter than lukewarm, add the yeast water.
4. Cap the jug and invert several times to mix. Then bottle and store in a dark place.
5. Check carbonation after 48 hours and again after 72 hours. When carbonation is right, refrigerate.

 Eleven 12-ounce bottles

Straight Fork Birch Beer

This recipe is named after my friend Ross Straight, whose ancestors in central West Virginia started a community with the seemingly contradictory name of Straight Fork. Ross lives in the same county as I do, but while my home has no black birch trees anywhere in the area, Ross's property is covered with them. Ross and his son Hans were kind enough to tap several birch trees for my use, and I was kind enough to bring them some homemade birch beer five days later. If you were to choose between leaving out either the twigs or the sap from the recipe, I would urge you to leave out the sap — the twigs contribute considerably more of the delicious wintergreen flavor.

> 1 quart black birch twigs (small ones!), fairly packed
> 15 inches fresh-dug sassafras root, the thickness of a pencil
> 3 to 4 quarts black birch sap
> 1¾ cups sugar
> ⅛ teaspoon ale yeast
> (also ¼ cup lukewarm water)

1. Place the twigs, roots, and sap in a pan and simmer, uncovered, for about 25 minutes.

2. Add sugar, and taste. If the sassafras taste is weak, add more sassafras; if the wintergreen taste is weak, add more birch twigs.

3. Remove from heat, cover, and let cool until lukewarm. (Submersing the pot in a clean sinkful of cold water is helpful; changing the cold water several times will hasten the cooling.) Move quickly when the liquid reaches lukewarm; at this stage it is most vulnerable to infections by wild yeasts or other tiny life-forms!

4. Reconstitute the dried yeast in ¼ cup lukewarm water, letting sit a few minutes, then add to the lukewarm sap mixture.

5. Strain the liquid into a glass jug, then pour into bottles and cap.

6. Leave at room temperature about 48 hours; when carbonation is right, refrigerate.

 Eleven 12-ounce bottles

Sarsaparilla Soda

Traditionally, sarsaparilla soda is made with sassafras root as well as sarsaparilla root. This raises the question of the best ratio of the two roots. My opinion is that although sarsaparilla is not delicious enough on its own to make an excellent soft drink, sassafras easily overpowers. What we want, then, is enough sassafras to make the overall taste delicious, but enough sarsaparilla to allow its nice flavor to come through as well. As always, specifying the proper amount of root is difficult because strength and aroma will vary from plant to plant, and drying and storage do take their toll. Use your eyes, nose, and taste buds to make a good combination of roots.

For many of us, our intro-duction to the word "sarsa-parilla" came from watch-ing cowboy movies and seeing the hero walk into the saloon and ask for "a nice tall sa's'parilla." None of us knew what a sarsapa-rilla was, of course, but we knew our hero didn't drink beer or whiskey!

In the eastern United States, sarsaparilla sodas were always less common than drinks made from the more readily available sas-safras, birch, and spruce trees. Arizona and New Mexico were closer to sources of sarsaparilla root (in Central America) than to plant products from the East Coast. Like sassafras, sarsaparilla was considered to be a general tonic, invigorating at once all the body's systems. Herbalists have also pre-scribed an infusion of the root for colds, fever, rheumatism, gout, and to aid in the passing of gas.

     3 to 4 **quarts water**
        9 **tablespoons chopped dried sarsaparilla root
(less if your supply is quite pungent)**
        5 **tablespoons chopped dried sassafras root bark
(more if your supply is not very pungent)**
      ¼ **cup raisins, coarsely chopped**
   1¾ **cups table sugar**
      ⅛ **teaspoon granulated ale yeast
(also ¼ cup lukewarm water)**

1. Heat 2 quarts of water to a simmer. As the water heats, add the chopped roots, chopped raisins, and sugar. Simmer, uncovered, for about 25 minutes. The color of the liquid should be a very deep red, and the familiar aroma of sassafras should be present, modi-fied by the somewhat less familiar aroma of sarsaparilla. If the color is weak or the aroma in the room is not very strong, add more sassafras and/or sarsaparilla. You may also wish to taste the brew, but remember that only about half the water has been added. If the sassafras taste is totally overpowering, add more sarsaparilla. If the sassafras taste is not very strong, add more sassafras.

2. Remove from heat, cover, and let cool. Put 1 quart of cool water into a jug.

3. After the sarsaparilla mixture has cooled 30 minutes, pour it slowly into the jug, straining as you pour. Now top off the jug, aiming for a lukewarm overall temperature. Discard the roots and raisins.

4. Cap the jug and agitate vigorously.

5. Put ¼ cup lukewarm water in a teacup and add the granulated yeast. Meanwhile, top off the jug, leaving about 2 inches of head-space at the top. Aim for an overall lukewarm temperature. (If the liquid ends up being hotter than lukewarm, allow it to cool with the cap on.)

6. Add the yeast water to the jug and agitate vigorously again. Bottle and let sit at room temperature.

7. Check the carbonation after 48 hours and again after 72 hours (sooner if the air temperature is especially warm). When the car-bonation is right, refrigerate.

 Eleven 12-ounce bottles

 An Alternative Method for Making Sarsaparilla

If you find yourself confused about the amount of root that will make a tasty beverage, you can simmer 4 quarts of water on the stove together with roots, raisins, and sugar. This will make it easier for you to devise a "tea" that tastes good to you and that will thus make an appetizing beverage. The disadvantage of this method is that the cooling will take considerably longer, and the danger of the beverage being "infected" with wild yeasts or other unwanted microorganisms increases.

One way to hurry the cooling process is to sit the covered pot in a clean sinkful of very cold water, changing the water bath whenever it is no longer cold. This way, the 4 quarts of liquid should be lukewarm within 30 minutes or so.

Virgin Islands Ginger Beer

My wife and I remember well our first taste of Virgin Islands Ginger Beer. We were visiting the National Folklife Festival at the Smithsonian Institution in Washington, DC. The festival showcased the Caribbean culture of the U.S. Virgin Islands, and the mall in front of the Capitol was dotted with food concessions featuring the cuisine of the islands. On prominent display was bottled ginger beer from St. Thomas, a little cloudy, and oh so strong in flavor. We resolved that one day we would make the recipe ourselves. A decade later, after I began regularly making soft drinks, I did my best to duplicate what we had tasted in Washington that day. This recipe is the result.

2$\frac{1}{2}$ ounces gingerroot
Juice of $\frac{1}{2}$ lemon
3 to 4 quarts water
1$\frac{2}{3}$ cups table sugar
$\frac{1}{8}$ teaspoon ale yeast (baker's yeast, as always, will work in a pinch; also $\frac{1}{4}$ cup lukewarm water)

1. Grate the gingerroot coarsely into the brewpot, using a kitchen grater. Squeeze the juice from the half lemon into the brewpot. Add 2 quarts of water and bring to a simmer. Add the sugar, stirring until it dissolves. Simmer, uncovered, for about 25 minutes, then remove from heat, cover, and let cool.

2. Put 1 quart of cool water into a jug. After the ginger mixture has cooled 30 minutes, pour slowly into the jug.

3. Now top off the jug, aiming for a lukewarm overall temperature. Leave about 2 inches of headspace at the top of the jug.

4. Cap the jug and agitate vigorously. (If the liquid's temperature is hotter than lukewarm, be sure to allow it to cool to lukewarm.)

5. Put the yeast in a teacup, and add $\frac{1}{4}$ cup lukewarm water. Let sit about 5 minutes, then add to the mixture in the jug.

6. Cap the jug and agitate vigorously.

7. Bottle, using bottling instructions on page 34.

 Eleven 12-ounce bottles

Chinese Ginger Beer

I make no pretense of knowing what kind of ginger beer the residents of Beijing drink. Still, this beverage does a nice job of combining two flavors that are often found in Chinese restaurants: ginger and orange. Why not make up a batch to complement your next stir-fry? And for a bit of showmanship, try this: Use clear glass beer bottles, preferably with no logo painted on. Into the bottom of each bottle, at bottling time, place a red maraschino cherry, which will soon be surrounded by a snowy bed of yeast. The effect is, well, unusual, and will confirm to the world that you have too much free time on your hands.

> 2 ounces gingerroot, coarsely grated
> 1 tablespoon fresh lemon juice
> 2 teaspoons orange extract (from spice counter)
> 3 to 4 quarts water
> 1¾ cups sugar
> ⅛ teaspoon ale yeast (also ¼ cup lukewarm water)

Variation

To give orange color to the drink, add 12 drops of yellow food coloring and 4 drops of red.

1. Grate the ginger coarsely into the brewpot, using a kitchen grater. Add the lemon juice, orange extract, and 2 quarts of the water, and simmer, uncovered, for about 20 minutes. Remove from heat and add the sugar, stirring until dissolved. Cover and let cool for 30 minutes.

2. Pour 1 quart cool water into a jug. Pour the ginger liquid slowly into the jug. Top off with water, aiming for a lukewarm overall temperature; leave about 2 inches of headspace at the top of the jug. (If the temperature of the liquid in the jug is hotter than lukewarm, be sure to allow it to cool.)

3. In a teacup, combine the yeast and ¼ cup lukewarm water. Let sit about 5 minutes, then add to the jug.

4. Agitate, then pour into the clean bottles and cap.

5. Allow to sit at room temperature about 48 hours. When carbonation is right, refrigerate.

Eleven 12-ounce bottles

Ginger Lager

This recipe takes a first step toward experimenting with yeasts, by making a soft drink from lager yeast instead of ale yeast. The taste of this Ginger Lager will be somewhat different from the taste of ginger ales, and the lager flavor is augmented by the use of traditional lager hops. The only thing that prevents this from being a real German-style lager is the lack of grain taste and the lack of alcohol. Judged on its own merits, this is a refreshing drink with the bite of ginger and the bitterness of hops — just the thing to help you cool down after a hot day of lawn mowing or softball practice.

☞ Ale or Lager?

Why is it always ginger *ale?* Those familiar with beers know that there are two great categories of malted beverages, ales and lagers. These two types of beer have a markedly different flavor, chiefly because they are brewed with two different types of yeast. Ale yeasts were most popular in England, hence many early American brewing recipes were for ales — including the well-known ginger ale.

1¾ ounces fresh gingerroot, coarsely grated
1¾ cups sugar
3 to 4 quarts water
¼ ounce plus 1 teaspoon Hallertauer hop
   pellets (or other mild lager hops)
⅛ teaspoon granulated lager yeast
   (also ¼ cup lukewarm water)

1. Into the brewpot place the grated ginger, sugar, and 2 quarts of the water and bring to a simmer.
2. Add the ¼ ounce of hop pellets and simmer, uncovered, for 20 minutes. Remove pot from heat and add the 1 additional teaspoon of hop pellets (this will replace some of the hop aroma that may have been destroyed by boiling). Allow to cool, covered, for 30 minutes.
3. Into a jug place 2 quarts of cool water. Slowly pour contents of the brewpot into the jug, straining as you pour.
4. Into a teacup, place ¼ cup lukewarm water and the lager yeast. Make absolutely certain that the temperature of the jug contents is not hotter than lukewarm, then add the yeast water.
5. Cap and invert several times to mix.
6. Bottle. With this recipe you should make sure not to set the bottles in too warm a location — lager yeasts are happiest working at temperatures of 40–66°F.
7. Check carbonation after 72 hours. When the carbonation is right, refrigerate.

 Eleven 12-ounce bottles

Ten-Root Spring Tonic

4 quarts water

4 ounces dried small spikenard (wild sarsaparilla) root

4 ounces dried dandelion root

¼ ounce dried sassafras root

5 inches dried Queen Anne's lace (wild carrot) root

4 teaspoons dried, chopped yellow (curled) dock root

2 teaspoons dried, chopped burdock root

4 teaspoons dried, chopped American ginseng root (or substitute an Asian form)

4 teaspoons dried, chopped chicory root

4 teaspoons dried, chopped licorice root

4 teaspoons dried, chopped sarsaparilla root

4 teaspoons dried saw palmetto berries

4 teaspoons dried smooth sumac (dwarf sumac) berries

4 teaspoons crushed, dried common juniper berries

1¾ cups sugar (or scant 1½ cups honey)

⅛ teaspoon granulated ale yeast (also ¼ cup lukewarm water)

1. Place 2 quarts of water into the brewpot and add all herbal ingredients and the sugar. Simmer, uncovered, for 10 minutes. Then cover, remove from heat, and allow to steep for 30 minutes more.
2. Pour the remaining 2 quarts of cool water into a 1-gallon glass jug, then strain in the contents of the brewpot.
3. Place the ale yeast into a teacup containing the ¼ cup of lukewarm water and allow to sit for several minutes.
4. After verifying that the contents of the jug are not hotter than lukewarm, add the yeast water.
5. Cap the jug and invert several times to mix. Then bottle, and store in a dark place.
6. Check carbonation after 48 hours and again after 72 hours. As soon as carbonation is right, refrigerate.

 Eleven 12-ounce bottles

Note: Fresh herbal ingredients may be substituted for the dried; use about one-third more.

 Toning Tonic

This recipe includes the roots of eight plants native to the United States, imported licorice and sarsaparilla roots, and the seeds of three native plants. While each herbal ingredient is present in a very small amount, collectively the effect is that of a good spring tonic — a gentle strengthener of all the body's systems. Be assured that leaving out two or three ingredients will have little effect on the overall tonic properties of this drink. If you omit the sassafras, add plenty of some other especially good-tasting ingredient, such as birch twigs or mint leaves.

Lemon-Lime Soda

I guess I was never much of an all-American kid, because I never liked colas. On trips, whenever my family stopped at the filling station, everyone else would choose a cola while I put my dime in the machine for America's best-selling lemon-lime soda. The slogan of this product in those days was "You like it, It likes you." At age 7 I was delighted to have anyone, or anything, like me. I'm sure you'll like the drink described below — though in all honesty, I can't say how the drink will feel about you.

Variations

This recipe produces a cloudy drink that is pleasantly sour, like lemonade. If you prefer a sweeter drink, omit 1 lemon and be a little more generous in measuring out the 2 cups of sugar. If you object to seeing pulp floating in your soft drink bottle, strain the juice before adding it to the jug. Straining will also make it easier to clean your bottles for their next use.

3 to 4 quarts water
Scant 2 cups sugar
2 lemons
5 limes
1/8 teaspoon granulated ale yeast (also 1/4 cup lukewarm water)

1. Heat 2 quarts of the water and the sugar, on very low heat. Stir until the sugar is dissolved. Cover and remove from heat.
2. Put 1 quart cool water into a 1-gallon glass jug. Pour the sugar mixture slowly into the jug.
3. Juice the fruits, then pour the juice into the jug. Top off the jug with water, leaving about 2 inches of headspace at the top of the jug. Aim for a lukewarm temperature of the liquid, adjusting the temperature of the water you are adding as needed.
4. Add the yeast to 1/4 cup lukewarm water in a teacup and allow to sit for 5 minutes.
5. Now add the yeast liquid to the jug and agitate vigorously.
6. Let sit in the loosely capped jug about 2 hours, in a warm place, then tighten cap and agitate some more.
7. Bottle and leave at room temperature. Because of the naturally occurring acids in the fruit, carbonation is very slow for this recipe, six to eight days is typical.
8. When carbonation is right, refrigerate.

Eleven 12-ounce bottles

Mint Lime Cooler

Millions of American families have spearmint growing on their land. Often they are oblivious to its presence, since the mint was planted decades earlier by a previous resident who had a penchant for iced tea. In other cases the mint sprang forth as an act of God, a particularly fragrant weed. If you don't have spearmint, see if you can beg, steal, or borrow from a friend several clumps for transplanting.

This recipe combines two flavors that are particularly noted for their cooling, thirst-quenching qualities: lime and mint. For an added pucker, a touch of lemon juice does the trick. Three hours before indulging, put a few glass mugs in the freezer. Serve this drink in frosted mugs with plenty of ice, and a sprig of mint leaves floating around for show.

> 5 sprigs fresh spearmint, each about 10 inches long
> 3 to 4 quarts water
> Juice of 5 limes (about $2/3$ cup juice)
> 1 tablespoon fresh lemon juice
> $1^3/4$ cups sugar
> $1/8$ teaspoon granulated ale yeast (also $1/4$ cup lukewarm water)

1. Place mint sprigs in a Mason jar or in a pan. Pour in 2 quarts of boiling water, cover, and allow to steep for 1 hour.
2. Put 1 quart of water into a glass jug, then add the lime juice and lemon juice.
3. Remove mint from its water. Stir sugar into the minty water, continuing to stir until sugar is dissolved.
4. Add this liquid to the liquid in the jug. Top off jug with water of the appropriate temperature to make overall jug contents lukewarm. Leave a little room at the top for the yeast water.
5. Put $1/4$ cup lukewarm water into a teacup, then add the granulated ale yeast. Add to jug, cap, and invert to mix.
6. Bottle, then store in a dark place.
7. With its fairly high concentration of citrus juices, this beverage will take longer than most to carbonate — about five to seven days is typical. When carbonation is right, refrigerate.

 Eleven 12-ounce bottles

 Variations

Replace the spearmint with peppermint, and create a soft drink that not only will taste good but also will help when you have a cold. The vitamin C will be of benefit, and good strong peppermint can help clear your sinuses. Or replace the spearmint with catnip (another member of the mint family) to create a beverage even the family cat will enjoy — if your cat likes lime, that is.

Cherry-Lemon Soda

1 gallon cherry juice (buy a fruit juice blend with cherry as the dominant flavor; be sure to buy a product that contains 100 percent fruit juices)
2 tablespoons plus 1 teaspoon fresh lemon juice
1/8 teaspoon granulated ale yeast (also 1/4 cup lukewarm water)

Each year American orchards produce 333,000 tons of cherries. A sizable percentage of this cherry crop ends up in fruit juice blends, but carbonated cherry drinks are surprisingly hard to find. This recipe (and its variations) begins with a cherry juice blend. The blends commonly sold are a mixture of apple, pear, cherry, grape, and/or lemon, but in any event should be 100 percent fruit juice. You can find these blends at the supermarket with the canned, bottled, or frozen juices. Each of the four recipes here adds another ingredient or two to the fruit juice to provide a point of special interest. The more patient beverage maker can easily modify these recipes to include the use of fresh-pressed, unblended cherry juice. Whatever recipe you choose, the result will be a beverage satisfying in flavor, thirst quenching, and startlingly brilliant in color.

1. If your fruit juice is chilled, allow to come to room temperature in a sealed container. Alternatively, heat to room temperature on the stove top.
2. Put fruit juice (including the lemon juice) into a 1-gallon glass jug.
3. Place granulated ale yeast in a teacup with the 1/4 cup lukewarm water and allow to sit for several minutes.
4. Add the yeast water to the jug, and cap. Turn jug over several times to mix.
5. Bottle, and store in a dark place.
6. Test carbonation after 48 hours and again after 72 hours. When carbonation is right, refrigerate.

 Eleven 12-ounce bottles

Cherry Vanilla Soda

1 cup water
4 tablespoons brown sugar
4 inches vanilla bean
1 gallon cherry juice (buy a fruit juice blend
    with cherry as the dominant flavor; be sure
    the product contains 100 percent fruit juices)
1/8 teaspoon granulated ale yeast (also 1/4 cup
    lukewarm water)

1. Put water, sugar, vanilla bean, and 2 cups of the cherry juice into a small pan, heat to just below boiling, and simmer, uncovered, for about 15 minutes. Stir occasionally until sugar dissolves.
2. Remove from heat, cover, and allow to sit for about 20 minutes more.
3. Pour remaining cherry juice (at room temperature) into a jug, then add the contents of the pan.
4. Put ale yeast into a teacup with the 1/4 cup lukewarm water and allow to sit several minutes, then pour the yeasty water into the jug. Cap the jug and invert it several times to mix.
5. Bottle, then store in a dark place.
6. Test carbonation after 48 hours and again after 72 hours. When carbonation is right, refrigerate.

 Eleven 12-ounce bottles

Cherry Sassafras Soda

2 quarts cherry juice (buy a fruit juice blend with cherry as the dominant flavor; be sure the product contains 100 percent fruit juices)

2 quarts water

3/4 cup brown sugar, lightly packed

10 inches fresh sassafras root, the thickness of a pencil

1/8 teaspoon granulated ale yeast (also 1/4 cup lukewarm water)

1. If your fruit juice is chilled, allow to come to room temperature in a sealed container. Alternatively, heat to room temperature on the stove top.
2. In a medium-sized pan, place the water, brown sugar, and sassafras root. Bring to a simmer and continue simmering, uncovered, for about 25 minutes. Remove from heat and allow to sit with the pot lid on but ajar.
3. Put cherry juice into a 1-gallon glass jug.
4. After the sassafras mixture has cooled 20 minutes or so, add it to the glass jug.
5. Put ale yeast into a teacup containing the 1/4 cup lukewarm water and allow to sit for several minutes.
6. After ensuring that the overall temperature of the jug's contents is not hotter than lukewarm, add the yeast water. Cap the jug and invert to mix.
7. Bottle, and store in a dark place.
8. Check carbonation after 48 hours and again after 72 hours. As soon as carbonation is right, refrigerate.

 Eleven 12-ounce bottles

Cherry Cinnamon Soda

1 quart water
Scant 1/2 cup sugar
4 cinnamon sticks, each about 3 inches long
3 quarts cherry juice (buy a fruit juice blend
   with cherry as the dominant flavor; be sure
   the product contains 100 percent fruit juices)
1/8 teaspoon granulated ale yeast (also 1/4 cup
   lukewarm water)

1. Put water, sugar, cinnamon sticks, and 1 quart of the cherry juice
into a small pan and bring to a simmer. Continue to simmer,
uncovered, for about 15 minutes.

2. Remove from heat, cover, and let sit for about 30 minutes.

3. Pour the remaining cherry juice (at room temperature) into a
1-gallon glass jug, then add contents of the pan, straining as
you pour.

4. Put ale yeast into a teacup with the 1/4 cup lukewarm water and
allow to sit several minutes.

5. Verify that the jug contents are no hotter than lukewarm, then
pour the yeast water into the jug. Cap the jug and invert it several
times to mix.

6. Bottle, then store in a dark place.

7. Test carbonation after 48 hours and again after 72 hours; as soon
as carbonation is right, refrigerate.

 Eleven 12-ounce bottles

Maraschino Fizz

I find that this drink is just the thing for a hot July afternoon, being reminiscent of pink lemonade and even bringing back childhood memories of ice-cream treats topped with maraschino cherries. This drink will be cloudy and contains pulp. If you use a fine strainer or cheesecloth as you add the lemon juice to the jug, the beverage will be clearer and the bottles easier to clean.

There is an almost forgotten type of cordial called maraschino, made from the black, bitter wild cherry known as marasca. The cherries, the cordial, and good natural sources of maraschino flavor are all hard to come by.

In devising the recipe for Maraschino Fizz, I tried maraschino extract purchased from a dealer of wine-making supplies. I also purchased a bottle of maraschino syrup from the supermarket. Neither flavoring yielded a delicious beverage. In desperation, I tried the liquid from a bottle of red maraschino cherries. This yielded the best results. Admittedly the cherry liquid contains artificial as well as natural flavors and colors, but in the small quantities per bottle of drink, I don't believe you need be concerned about these flavors and colors.

3 to 4 quarts water
1¾ cups table sugar
Juice of 5 lemons
Liquid from a 10-ounce bottle of red maraschino cherries
¼ teaspoon granulated ale yeast
(also ¼ cup lukewarm water)

1. Heat 2 quarts of water on low heat, stirring in the sugar until dissolved. Remove water from heat and cover.
2. Put the juice of 5 lemons into a 1-gallon glass jug. Use a funnel to add the sugary water to the jug, then add the liquid from the jar of maraschino cherries. Cap the jug and agitate well.
3. Add water to the jug until it is nearly full, leaving about 2 inches of headspace at the top of the jug. Aim for an overall liquid temperature in the jug of lukewarm. (If the temperature is hotter than lukewarm, allow the contents of the jug to cool with the cap on.)
4. Put ¼ cup of lukewarm water in a teacup. Add the granulated yeast and let sit about 5 minutes.
5. Add the yeast water to the jug and agitate the jug vigorously. Put the jug in a warm place and allow to work about 2 hours.
6. Bottle the drink and put in a warm place. This drink will take longer to carbonate than drinks that do not contain large amounts of citrus juice — seven to ten days is typical, depending on the quality of yeast used, the room temperature, and the amount of juice produced by the lemons.
7. As soon as the carbonation is right, refrigerate.

 Eleven 12-ounce bottles

White Tigers

My family is from Mississippi, where not only iced tea but also iced coffee (with milk) was a tradition of long standing. In the early 1980s, my capitalist juices flowing during the Reagan years, I developed the idea of bottling iced coffee and stocking it in drink machines along the interstates. My new product, White Tigers, would allow travelers to avoid sugary drinks and would give them the added bit of wakefulness they were seeking. No more waiting for the coffee to cool! Needless to say, I never acted on this idea, and a couple of years ago a company did begin to market cold coffee in bottles.

My White Tigers will never reach the marketplace, but they are easy to make at home. I like to concoct a batch before a long trip or before a major construction day around our house. The drink is not carbonated, but its being bottled makes it easy to manage when you have driving — or pounding nails — on your mind. White Tigers are also a nice bottled drink to have at parties, for designated drivers or others who prefer not to drink beer.

> 2 inches vanilla bean
> Fresh-ground coffee (the amount of coffee you usually use for a full pot)
> 10 coffee cups of cold water
> 5 teaspoons sugar
> 3/4 cup whole milk

1. Put vanilla bean into the carafe before making the coffee. Then make the coffee as usual, allowing it to sit about 10 minutes before removing from the heat. Don't overheat the coffee!
2. Cool for 10 minutes.
3. Remove the vanilla bean, then add sugar and milk. Pour into bottles and cap.

 Eleven 12-ounce bottles

 Variations

Plain White Tigers: Omit vanilla bean.

Cinnamon White Tigers: Replace the vanilla bean with about 2 inches of stick cinnamon.

Creole White Tigers: Replace the sugar with 2 teaspoons light molasses.

Kitchen Sink White Tigers: Use vanilla bean, cinnamon, and molasses (but no sugar).

Black White Tigers: I encourage even lovers of black coffee to try this drink with the suggested milk and modest amount of sugar. A plain black White Tiger is theoretically possible but not likely to be a crowd pleaser.

▼ Cream Soda

No book of soft drink recipes would be complete without one for cream soda. Unfortunately, the origin of this soft drink is lost in the mists of history. A favorite in kosher delicatessens in New York City, this drink was also found regularly on the tables of well-to-do families of the American South in the nineteenth century. Experts can't even seem to agree on what a cream soda is. In some recipes the "cream" refers to table cream, while in others the only cream is cream of tartar — a chemical best known as an ingredient in baking powder. Still other recipes include creamy, beaten egg whites and even white flour. The strongest evidence I have found shows that the earliest cream soda was simply a vanilla-flavored soda; at serving time, a dollop of cream was added to each glass. Let this recipe be a starting point for you in your quest for the ultimate cream soda.

> ¼ cup raisins, coarsely chopped
> 6 inches vanilla bean
> 4 quarts water
> 3 inches cinnamon bark
> 1¾ cups brown sugar, gently packed
> ¼ teaspoon cream of tartar
> ⅛ teaspoon granulated ale yeast (also ¼ cup lukewarm water)

1. Place the raisins in the brewpot. Add the vanilla bean, 2 quarts of water, the cinnamon, and the sugar, and simmer, uncovered, for 20 minutes.
2. Remove from heat. Stir in the cream of tartar, blending until dissolved.
3. Cover, then let cool for about 30 minutes.
4. Place 2 quarts of cool water in a 1-gallon glass jug. Add contents of the brewpot, straining as you pour.
5. Place the ale yeast in a teacup with the ¼ cup of lukewarm water and allow to sit a few minutes.
6. Verify that the temperature of the jug's contents is not hotter than lukewarm, then add the yeast water to the jug.

7. Bottle, then store in a dark place.
8. Check the carbonation after 48 hours and again after 72 hours. When carbonation is right, refrigerate.

 Eleven 12-ounce bottles

To serve, add a dollop of fresh table cream to each glass. How much is a dollop? Expert cooks refuse to divulge this information, but try about 2 tablespoons per glass.

 A Wintergreen Variation

Add 6 drops of oil of wintergreen to the mixture after adding the cream of tartar. Or add one or two of the tiny leaves of wild wintergreen to each bottle.

Kvass

Mention traditional American homemade beverages, and most people will think of the sassafras root beers once made in the isolated hollers of Appalachia — or maybe the corn whiskey made in these same hollers. But American folk culture goes far beyond the Scotch-Irish traditions most common in America's eastern mountains. In her cities, many Russian and Eastern European immigrants — Jews, Catholics, and Russian Orthodox — brought their beverage-making traditions with them. Few beverages are more distinctive than kvass, a lightly carbonated and only slightly alcoholic Russian beverage. A number of homebrewers making kvass have reported that they didn't find it very tasty. This may be because kvass is unlike anything we are used to.

Start with black bread soaked in boiling water. Add raisins, mint, and yeast, and you have — well, a far cry from our more familiar soft drinks. Still, the tens of thousands of Russians who continued to make kvass each year after coming to this country testify that there is something important about this drink. To them it's a pleasant and familiar taste; to others, perhaps it's a window to another culture. Try some kvass the next time you feel adventurous.

>   1 pound black bread
>   2 sprigs of peppermint, each 12 inches long
>   5 quarts boiling water
> 2½ cups sugar
>   ⅛ teaspoon granulated ale yeast (also ¼ cup
>   lukewarm water)
>   Small handful sultanas

1. Slice the bread and toast the slices lightly on each side.
2. Place the bread into a gauze or cheesecloth bag (or fashion a bag with safety pins and a kitchen towel).
3. Put the mint into a large crock or a large stainless-steel pan, then set the bread bag on top of the mint. Pour boiling water over the bread bag, cover, and let sit for 6 hours.
4. Remove the bread bag and let drip into the container for 30 minutes.
5. Squeeze the bag gently to recapture most of the water. Put the liquid on the stove and heat on low, taking care not to get it hotter

than lukewarm. Stir in the sugar and continue stirring until dissolved. Remove the mint.

6. Place the ¼ cup lukewarm water into a teacup and add the ale yeast. After a few minutes, pour the yeast water into the container with the sugary liquid. Allow to sit, covered, about 8 hours.

7. Pour the liquid into a 1-gallon glass jar. Place 2 or 3 sultanas in the bottom of each bottle. Fill from the jug and cap. Store bottles in a dark location.

8. Check carbonation after 36 hours. When carbonation is right, refrigerate.

 Thirteen 12-ounce bottles

To reduce the alcohol level from quite modest to barely any, bottle immediately after adding the yeast.

 Variations

Try kvass without mint, or kvass made from rye bread instead of black bread. Also, do as Russian peasants did, and use the kvass as a stock for soups.

Switchels, Shrubs, Vinegar Drinks, and Mulled Beverages

Whenthe leaves began to turn orange and a chill was in the air, farm wives across the country turned their attention to harvest drinks. It was critical to have on hand thirst-quenching, rehydrating, nonintoxicating beverages as neighbors and hired help showed up to work long hours at the harvest. Many traditional harvest drinks had vinegar as a key ingredient, substituting it for the rum or brandy that was present in even older recipes.

Switchel

Switchel is a beverage flavored with molasses, ginger, and vinegar. The word is American, but etymologists seem to have no idea of its derivation. They can only surmise that it may have the same origin as swizzle, as in swizzle stick. A 1790 entry in the *New York Daily Advertiser,* apparently referring to a local night spot, promised that the visitor would quaff pleasant beverages, "not wretched switchel and vile hogo drams." "Hogo," by the way, means putrescent in flavor. In the recipes that follow we aim to ensure that our switchels are not vile, our drams not hogo.

Shrubs and Mulled Drinks

Shrubs are fruit drinks with a bit of tang provided by vinegar or by the addition of an alcoholic beverage such as brandy. They are easy to make — they are simply mixed, not brewed — but have really nice thirst-quenching properties. Mulled drinks are fruit juices that have been flavored with spices such as cinnamon and cloves. Mulled drinks are not really brewed but are heated gently to bring out the flavor of the spices. Note that many of the recipes in this chapter are for non-carbonated drinks, but all may be bottled and capped for effortless serving later. Also, the recipes for noncarbonated drinks are easily modified to make the drink carbonated, if you prefer.

Raspberry Shrub

In the nineteenth century, cool places on the farm were at a premium. Yet cold storage even of noncarbonated beverages was a necessity, since at room temperature spoilage was likely, especially if fruit juice was one of the ingredients. Recipes such as this one produced a concentrated drink that would occupy little room in the springhouse, but made quite a bit of drink when mixed with water. The presence of vinegar helped prevent spoilage and also added a pleasant bite that sometimes seemed to be missing from more tame, nonalcoholic beverages.

> 2 cups raspberries (fresh or frozen)
> 1/2 cup white wine vinegar
> 2 cups sugar

1. Place raspberries in a small pot, then cover with vinegar and mash with a potato masher. Begin heating on low heat, adding the sugar gradually until all of it has been dissolved. Bring to a boil and then remove from heat.

2. Strain into another vessel, allowing to drip so as to extract as much liquid as possible. Allow to cool somewhat, but pour into a bottle just before it reaches lukewarm temperature. Refrigerate.

3. *To make a glass of drink:* Stir 1/4 cup of the mixture into a glass of water, then add ice.

 Twelve to fourteen servings

Molasses Switchel

While many harvest drinks relied on fruit juices, switchel was a spicy, vinegary drink without fruit juice. It proved unusually thirst-quenching, and aided digestion after the heavy harvest meals. The switchel served during the work of harvest was nonalcoholic, meaning that the harvest hands could successfully negotiate the evening dance that followed the elaborate picnic, or "supper on the ground." Although switchel was noncarbonated as well as nonalcoholic, the traditional recipes may be modified to create a carbonated drink, if desired.

3 to 4 quarts water
1/2 cup apple cider vinegar
1 1/2 cups sugar
1/3 cup light molasses
2 ounces fresh grated gingerroot

1. Combine 1 quart of the water, the vinegar, sugar, molasses, and gingerroot and simmer, uncovered. Remove from heat, cover, and allow to cool for about 30 minutes.
2. Pour slowly into a glass jug containing 2½ quarts of water. Top off with water to make 1 gallon.
3. *For a traditional noncarbonated switchel:* Chill immediately. Bottling and capping is optional.
4. *For a carbonated drink:* Place 1/8 teaspoon granulated ale yeast into a teacup containing 1/4 cup lukewarm water and allow to rehydrate a few minutes. After verifying that the temperature in the jug is not hotter than lukewarm, add the yeast water to the jug, cap, and invert to mix the contents. Bottle, then store the bottles in a dark place. Check carbonation after 48 hours and again after 72 hours. When the carbonation is right, refrigerate.

 Eleven 12-ounce bottles

Molasses Beer

*Recipe of
Elizabeth E. Lea
Published at Baltimore,
1869*

Take five pints of molasses, half a pint of yeast, two spoonsful of pounded ginger, and one of allspice; put these into a clean half-barrel, and pour on it two gallons of boiling water; shake it till a fermentation is produced; then fill it up with warm water, and let it work with the bung out, a day, when it will be fit for use; remove it to a cold place, or bottle it. This is a very good drink for laboring people in warm weather.

Mulled Ginger Apple Ale

This recipe is a nice combination of two drinks that almost everyone seems to like: a ginger ale soft drink and mulled apple cider. Alternative instructions are given for making this drink carbonated, like a ginger ale, or noncarbonated, like a mulled cider Christmas punch. Either way, the flavors are evocative of the first bite of cold weather and the smell of an oak wood fire.

2 quarts water
2 quarts apple juice
2 ounces grated fresh gingerroot
6 cinnamon sticks (each about 3 inches long)
15 cloves
A few slivers from a whole nutmeg
(or ¼ teaspoon fresh grated nutmeg)
½ teaspoon dried orange peel
Scant 1 cup sugar

1. Put 1 quart each of the water and apple juice into a pot, together with the spices and sugar. Simmer, uncovered, for 15 minutes and remove from heat. Cover and let cool for about 20 minutes.

2. Put the remaining 1 quart each of water and apple juice into a 1-gallon glass jug. Add the liquid from the brewpot to the liquid in the jug, straining out the spices as you pour.

3. *To use as a traditional mulled cider:* Refrigerate immediately. Bottle and cap, if desired.

4. *To make a carbonated drink:* Put ⅛ teaspoon granulated ale yeast into a teacup with ¼ cup of lukewarm water and allow to rehydrate several minutes. Verify that the temperature of the liquid in the jug is no hotter than lukewarm, then pour the yeast water into the jug. Cap, then invert the jug several times to mix. Bottle, then store in a dark place. Check the carbonation after 48 hours and again after 72 hours. When carbonation is right, refrigerate.

Eleven 12-ounce bottles

Elderflower Champagne

Despite its name, this recipe is for a soft drink, and children will enjoy helping to gather the flowers, brew the beverage, and drink the finished product. While this is a drink of springtime rather than the harvest, it is included here among the beverages containing vinegar as an important ingredient. Put elderflower champagne on your calendar for June, when whole hillsides light up with the flowers of elder shrubs. Be sure to leave some flowers behind — to feed the bees and butterflies, and to allow elderberries to form for the use of birds and wine makers.

 Elder Borer

Folk entomologists should keep watch for the magnificent elder borer, a large and beautiful longhorn beetle in shades of metallic blue and school bus yellow. The borers will be feeding on top of the flower, along with a host of other diminutive life-forms attracted by the flower's strong scent. Budget an hour or so for separating pollen-feeding insects from the flower heads before you begin brewing.

For an added touch, put up this drink in champagne bottles, closed either with regular caps or with traditional mushroom-shaped corks and wire closures.

> 3 to 4 **quarts water**
> 1 **ounce ginger, grated**
> 1 **quart elderflower heads**
> **Juice of 1 lemon**
> 4 **teaspoons white wine vinegar**
> **Scant 2 cups sugar**
> 1/8 **teaspoon granulated ale yeast**
> **(also 1/4 cup lukewarm water)**

1. Heat the water and grated ginger; simmer, uncovered, for 20 minutes and remove from heat. Allow to cool for 10 minutes.

2. Add the flowers, lemon juice, and vinegar. Cover and let sit for 12 hours.

3. Heat slightly (to lukewarm only), adding the sugar. Stir until sugar dissolves. Remove from heat and cover.

4. Put yeast into a teacup with 1/4 cup of lukewarm water; allow to rehydrate for about 5 minutes. Add to the pot of lukewarm liquid.

5. Strain into a 1-gallon glass jug, then pour into clean bottles and cap.

6. Check carbonation after 48 hours; refrigerate when carbonation is sufficient.

 Eleven 12-ounce bottles

Mulled Grapeade

While nearly everyone has enjoyed the taste of mulled apple cider in the late fall or at Christmastime, mulled grape juice is a considerably rarer treat. If you have home-grown grapes and a fruit press, the mulled beverage you create can be astoundingly good. Even from bottled, canned, or reconstituted grape juice, the taste will be excellent. Try this drink at your next holiday gathering.

4 quarts fresh pressed grape juice (or 3$\frac{1}{2}$ quarts other grape juice plus 1 pint water)
$\frac{1}{2}$ ounce coarsely grated ginger
12 cinnamon sticks (each about 3 inches long)
15 cloves
A few slivers from a whole nutmeg (or $\frac{1}{4}$ teaspoon fresh grated nutmeg)
$\frac{1}{2}$ teaspoon dried orange peel

1. Put 2 quarts of the juice into a pot together with the spices. Simmer, uncovered, for 15 minutes and remove from heat. Cover and let cool for about 30 minutes.

2. Meanwhile, put the remaining liquid into a 1-gallon glass jug. Add the liquid from the brewpot to the liquid in the jug, straining out the spices as you pour.

3. *To use as a traditional mulled drink:* Refrigerate immediately. Bottle and cap, if desired.

4. *To make a carbonated drink:* Put $\frac{1}{8}$ teaspoon granulated ale yeast into a teacup with $\frac{1}{4}$ cup of lukewarm water and allow to rehydrate several minutes. Verify that the temperature of the liquid in the jug is no hotter than lukewarm, then pour the yeast water into the jug. Cap, then invert the jug several times to mix. Bottle, then store in a dark place. Check the carbonation after 48 hours and again after 72 hours. Refrigerate as soon as the carbonation is right.

 Eleven 12-ounce bottles

▼ Dandelion Champagne

One of the satisfactions of home beverage making is converting a yardful of weeds into a delicious and satisfying drink. While finding a sufficient quantity of the dandelion flower heads is rarely a problem, do find a source where herbicides have not been used.

When my wife first made dandelion wine from a traditional recipe, I suspected the wine tasted good only because it was full of flavorful ingredients found in any kitchen, including oranges and various spices. My friend Mike Tawes, however, proved that the dandelions do provide a very strong and pleasant flavor, as his jar of dandelion wine had no extraneous ingredients (see chapter 2). This recipe is a modification of a recipe for dandelion wine. The beverage produced will be nonalcoholic, but I call it champagne because of the sharp carbonation that is present. A little vinegar restores some of the "bite" lost by the absence of alcohol. Herbalists consider dandelion a tonic, so expect a spring in your step after drinking a bottle or two of this leonine beverage.

1 gallon dandelion blossoms
1 cup raisins, coarsely chopped
1 lemon, cut in quarters
1 grapefruit (scooped out fruit and juice only)
1/2 teaspoon dried orange rind
1 gallon boiling water
1 3/4 cups sugar
3 tablespoons vinegar
1/8 teaspoon granulated ale yeast (also 1/4 cup lukewarm water)

1. Place dandelion blossoms and raisins into a large crock or pot, then squeeze the lemon into the pot and add the remaining lemon rind and pulp. Also add the grapefruit and the orange rind.
2. Over all these ingredients, pour 1 gallon of boiling water and allow to steep, covered, for 1½ hours.
3. Add sugar and stir until dissolved. Strain into a 1-gallon jug, and ensure that the temperature of the liquid is not hotter than lukewarm.

4. Put the ale yeast into a teacup with the ¼ cup of lukewarm water and allow to sit several minutes to rehydrate.
5. Add the yeast to the jug, cap, and invert several times to mix.
6. Bottle, then store in a dark place.
7. Check carbonation after 72 hours and again after 96 hours. When carbonation is right, refrigerate.

 Eleven 12-ounce bottles

 Dandelion Origins

If we lay aside our prejudices against this common weed, we will have to admit that the dandelion is an attractive flower. While some may claim to see a lion's mane in the flower's outline, the venerable name of this plant actually refers to the shape of its leaves. In Middle English the plant was called *dent-delyon,* and in Old French it was *dent de lion,* or tooth of the lion. The jagged outline of the dandelion's leaves evokes the ferocity of the king of beasts.

Harvest Beer

This is a traditional harvest drink made in the traditional way. It is less controlled — and hence more unpredictable — than the preceding recipes. Still, it's fun to try doing things by a centuries-old method, and if you start with good ingredients, you're likely to get a delicious beverage. Note that although there are some similarities between this beverage and the soft drink recipes given earlier, this one will produce a beverage within which the alcohol may be noticeable — though in most cases it is substantially less than that found in light beers. On the other hand, it is like a soft drink in that gushing or exploding bottles are a possibility, so refrigerate the bottles as soon as the carbonation is right. Aim to drink the entire batch within about four weeks.

In reading the list of ingredients for this recipe, you will notice right away the lack of any granulated yeast. The yeast that creates the alcohol and the carbonation will be wild yeast — either from the air or from the apple peel and raisin skins. If you have a good source for unwaxed apples free of pesticides, or for organically grown raisins, by all means use them.

> 4 pounds apples, grated
> $1/2$ pound raisins, chopped
> 2 gallons cold water
> $2^3/4$ pounds sugar
> 2 inches stick cinnamon
> 1 teaspoon whole cloves

1. Put apples and chopped raisins into a crock together with the cold water. Cover with cheesecloth; stir once daily for one week.
2. After one week, strain and then pour over the sugar and spices. Stir well, cover, and allow to sit for 12 hours.
3. Strain and bottle, letting it work at room temperature for about 48 hours. Refrigerate as soon as sufficiently carbonated.

 Twenty-two 12-ounce bottles

Reminder: This beverage may have a noticeable alcohol content, though usually less than the amount found in a typical American beer.

Pumpkin Ale

Anonymous Recipe
United States, 1771

Receipt for Pompion Ale

Let the Pompion be beaten in a Trough and pressed as Apples. The expressed Juice is to be boiled in A Copper a considerable Time and carefully skimmed that there may be no Remains of the fibrous Part of the Pulp. After that Intention is answered let the Liquor be hopped, cooled, fermented, &c. as Malt Beer.

Halloween Root Beer

This is more a description of a tradition than a recipe. In Sunday schools in the Upper Midwest, it was customary at the annual picnic to serve a spooky kind of Halloween root beer, smoking like a witch's cauldron. The following instructions include the use of root beer extract, sugar, and cold water, plus dry ice. The dry ice creates the spooky smoke, chills the beverage, and even makes some carbonation as you stir. If you have a lot of energy, forgo the dry ice and use a real cooking pot, a real fire, and hunks of sassafras root. (The resulting drink will have no carbonation but will still be very tasty; some of it could be bottled for carbonated consumption later.) Any of these methods will be a hit with the kids, and before you know it you'll have created a tradition in your community.

> 2-ounce bottle root beer extract
> 8 cups sugar
> Water to make 4½ gallons
> 5 pounds dry ice

1. In a very large pot or crock, mix the extract, sugar, and water according to the above proportions, or follow the instructions that come with the extract (but omit the yeast).
2. When the sugar has dissolved, add the dry ice and stir for about 45 minutes, then serve. (Take care not to touch the dry ice or to let any get into the serving cups — it's so cold that it can burn the skin.)

 About 5 gallons of beverage

Mulled Black Walnut Cider

☞ **Nutting Stones**

Out in my yard in rural Upshur County, West Virginia, is an Indian "nutting stone" my wife discovered nearby. The depressions in the stone are perfectly designed for holding black walnuts so they can be struck with a heavy object. The nutting stone still works, and I get an ineffable feeling knowing that hundreds of years ago Native Americans enjoyed the groves of black walnut trees as much as I do, and that their useful tool is still employed by people who appreciate this delicious food. A nutting stone is almost required to prepare black walnuts; the process of dehusking, then cracking the extraordinarily hard shell, and finally picking out the nutmeats can be ludicrously time-consuming.

Black walnuts are one of those foods that people tend either to love or to hate. Like asparagus, broccoli, and anchovies, black walnuts can divide a family. Make a pan of brownies with black walnuts and chances are some of your family will be delighted while others wail, "Why couldn't you have used English walnuts?" To the black walnut fan, of course, an English walnut is a poor, flavorless substitute for the real thing. For connoisseurs of black walnuts, this recipe is for you.

1 gallon apple cider
2 sticks cinnamon (about 3–4 inches each)
18 cloves
3 tablespoons coarsely grated gingerroot
4 tablespoons sugar
2½ teaspoons black walnut extract

1. Put 2 quarts of the apple cider into a pot together with the spices and sugar. Simmer, uncovered, for 15 minutes and remove from heat. Cover and let cool for about 25 minutes.

2. Put the remaining 2 quarts of cider into a 1-gallon glass jug. Add the liquid from the brewpot to the liquid in the jug, straining out the spices as you pour. Add the walnut extract and mix well.

3. *To use as a traditional mulled cider:* Refrigerate immediately. Bottle and cap, if desired.

4. *To make a carbonated drink:* Put ⅛ teaspoon granulated ale yeast into a teacup with ¼ cup of lukewarm water and allow to rehydrate several minutes. Verify that the temperature of the liquid in the jug is no hotter than lukewarm, then pour the yeast water into the jug. Cap, then invert the jug several times to mix. Bottle, and store in a dark place. Check the carbonation after 48 hours and again after 72 hours. Refrigerate when carbonation is right.

 Eleven 12-ounce bottles

Wintertime Cinnamon Shrub

This drink, like all shrubs, begins with fruit juice. What is somewhat unusual about this recipe is that the juices derive from dried
fruits. It's a good beverage for wintertime making because you
don't have to worry about finding high-quality fresh fruit, and
because the bite of cinnamon and vinegar will keep you warm even
when the chill winds blow down from Saskatoon.

> 1/2 cup raisins, coarsely chopped
> 3 cups dried apples, chopped
> 5 sticks cinnamon, each 3 inches long
> 2 tablespoons apple cider vinegar
> 1 cup sugar
> 3 to 4 quarts water
> 1/8 teaspoon granulated ale yeast (also 1/4 cup
> lukewarm water)

1. Put the chopped raisins, dried apples, cinnamon stick, vinegar,
and sugar into the brewpot and heat to near simmering for 30
minutes. Keep stirring until the sugar is dissolved, then stir
occasionally.

2. Remove from heat and allow to cool, covered but with the lid ajar,
for 25 minutes.

3. Pour 2 quarts of cool water into a 1-gallon glass jug. Put 1/4 cup
lukewarm water into a teacup and add the ale yeast, allowing it to
rehydrate for several minutes.

4. Strain the sweet liquid slowly into the glass jug. Check the temperature, then top off the jug, leaving about 2 inches of headspace for the yeast water. Aim for an overall temperature of
lukewarm.

5. Add the yeast water, cap, and invert several times to mix. Bottle,
then store in a dark place.

6. Check carbonation after 48 hours and again after 72 hours.
Refrigerate when carbonation is right.

 Eleven 12-ounce bottles

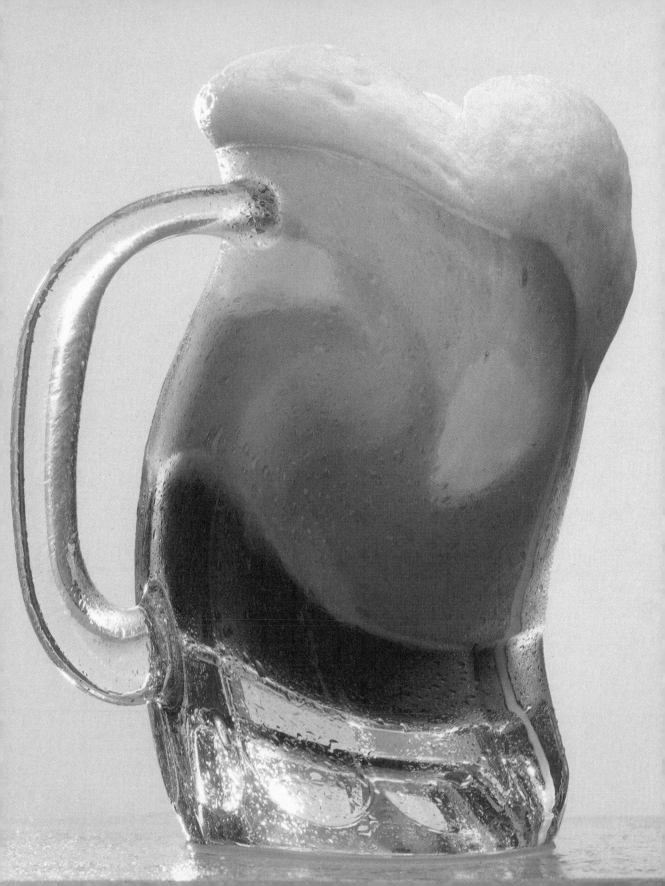

Ingredients for Devising Your Own Recipes

hese recipes make drinks far superior to those manufactured today by the huge conglomerates of the beverage industry. One difference you will notice is that the taste of yeast is present in homemade libations. Many people like this yeasty taste, and most others grow to appreciate it over time. Commercial drinks do not contain yeast; they are artificially carbonated with injections of carbon dioxide.

The root beers and other soft drinks described in this book are much less sweet than modern soft drinks. For most recipes, I find 1¾ cups of sugar per gallon is about right. Those with a sweet tooth may prefer 2 cups of sugar per gallon, and this is still less than is used in national brands of sodas. Those who have really cut down on sugar in their diets may prefer as little as 1½ cups per gallon. With ginger ale, many recipes call for 1 ounce of grated gingerroot per gallon; I often double or triple this amount for a beverage with a real "bite." The best thing about making soft drinks at home is that you can tailor recipes to your own tastes.

Making Your Own Recipes

Part of the fun of making beverages at home is devising your own recipes. What follows is a list of ingredients you might consider using, but please do not let the list limit your imagination.

YEAST

Yeasts are single-celled plants that, like mushrooms, are classed as fungi. Yeasts are in the air we breathe. Over the course of thousands of years, those who fermented beer and wine, and bakers who made bread, captured the wild yeasts and gradually improved the strains. Yeast is good for you, containing B-complex vitamins. In fact, some people buy brewer's yeast at the health food store to use as a beneficial food additive. Note, however, that the brewer's yeast sold at health food stores is no longer active and will not work for brewing beverages!

Beer yeasts. Remember to try not only granulated ale yeasts, but also granulated lager yeasts. Granulated lager yeasts are a little harder to find than granulated ale yeasts, and homebrewers sometimes complain about the poor quality of dried lager yeasts. If you prefer, invest a couple of dollars and purchase a lager "liquid yeast culture" from your homebrew supplier — to use, just follow the instructions on the package. Later, you can experiment with a couple of dozen varieties of liquid yeast cultures, including such exotics as traditional wheat beer yeasts. Each yeast will provide the finished beverage with a somewhat different taste.

Bread yeast. While I recommend granulated ale yeast for all soft drinks, bread yeast works, too, and will produce a good beverage. If you find yourself without ale yeast on brewing day, don't lose sleep over using bread yeast.

Champagne and wine yeasts. These work very well in soft drink recipes and will provide subtle shifts in flavor. Experiment to see which of these yeasts you prefer.

ROOTS

Tuber, taproot, rhizome, corm, bulb — a root by any other name would smell just about the same. Fragrance and flavor are the most important elements that roots add to a homemade beverage. Some roots also provide color, and some have healing and tonic properties.

Experimentation with liquid yeast cultures can result in the discovery of new soft drink recipes that produce beverages with a novel twang. Liquid yeast cultures come in a foil "smack pack" that looks like this.

Burdock root *(Arctium lappa)*. Burdock is a traditional ingredient in American root beers, taken from a purple-flowering plant common over much of the United States. The root is said to eliminate poisons from the body and has an essential oil that adds a very small amount of flavor. Start with 1 tablespoon of chopped root in 1 gallon of root beer, and modify the amount as desired in subsequent batches. If you're digging this plant yourself, be prepared for a real dig. This plant has an especially long taproot that goes straight down!

Gingerroot *(Zingiber officinale)*. This is a basic ingredient of many soft drinks. One to 3 ounces per gallon should be about right; use the smaller amount if the recipe has other flavors you want to come out or if you don't like a strong ginger "bite."

Licorice root *(Glycyrrhiza glabra)*. While not native to the United States, the root of the licorice plant is readily available in health food stores and from homebrew suppliers. It adds a unique flavor to beverages and also imparts a noticeable sweetness. For 1 gallon of root beer, use a 2- to 5-inch piece of root, depending on what other flavors are in your recipe. Some suppliers sell a "brewer's licorice stick," which is a manufactured product and not woody in appearance. I prefer the real root, but if you decide to use a brewer's licorice stick, use about one-third less than I recommend for the actual root.

Sarsaparilla root *(Smilax spp.)*. A number of plants around the world have "sarsaparilla" in their common name, but the usual sources for roots used in beverage making are several Latin American species of the genus *Smilax,* most commonly *S. regelii.* This is the same genus as the various greenbriers found in the United States, but the U.S. species are not appropriate for beverage making. The aroma of sarsaparilla is nice, not unlike sassafras. Seven to 10 tablespoons of chopped root per gallon of root beer should be appropriate. (Use less if the recipe contains other flavoring agents.)

Sassafras root *(Sassafras albidum)*. Traditionally a dominant flavor in root beers, this root is also found in sarsaparilla sodas and birch beers. Note that it is a very strong flavor that may not allow other flavors to shine through. If you are using several flavors in a soft drink, be careful not to overdo the sassafras root. A piece of root 20 inches long, and the thickness of a pencil, is about right for 1 gallon of root beer. Or use about ¼ ounce of dried root bark (red root bark that has been separated from the white wood of the root) per gallon. Sassafras root can be dried and reused, though with diminishing returns.

Ginger Pop

Recipe of
Mrs. Charles H. Gibson
Maryland, 1894

Two pounds brown sugar, one large tablespoonful of the fibrous part of ginger, half lemon sliced, one dessertspoon of cream of tarter, pour on it two gallons of boiling water, when milk warm stir in one pint brisk yeast; make it in the morning, bottle it at night. It will be ready for use in three days.

Sassafras Beer

Recipe of Miss Leslie
Published at Philadelphia, 1853

Have ready two gallons of soft water; one quart of wheat bran; a large handful of dried apples; half a pint of molasses; a small handful of hops; half a pint of strong fresh yeast, and a piece of sassafras root the size of an egg.

Put all the ingredients (except the molasses and yeast) at once into a large kettle. Boil it till the apples are quite soft. Put the molasses into a small clean tub or a large pan. Set a hair sieve over the vessel, and strain the mixture through it. Let it stand till it becomes only milkwarm, and then stir in the yeast. Put the liquor immediately into the keg or jugs, and let it stand uncorked to ferment. Fill the jugs quite full, that the liquor in fermenting may run over. Set them in a large tub. When you see that the fermentation or working has subsided, cork it, and it will be fit for use next day.

Two large table-spoonfuls of ginger stirred into the molasses will be found an improvement.

If the yeast is stirred in while the liquor is too warm, it will be likely to turn sour.

If the liquor is not put immediately into the jugs, it will not ferment well.

Keep it in a cold place. It will not in warm weather be good more than two days. It is only made for present use.

FRUIT

Perhaps you have preserved fruit before, by making canned or pickled fruits, jams, jellies, preserves, fruit butter, fruit leather, or sliced dried fruit. Now add to your repertoire one more method of preserving fruits: making soft drinks. You'll be preserving it all — the aroma, flavor, color, and nutritional values.

Citrus rinds. Try 2 to 5 tablespoons of chopped dried rind per gallon of soft drink, or experiment with fresh rinds. Avoid collecting the rind from citrus fruits that have been coated with various shiny products by the grocer. In cutting and drying rinds yourself, take only the zest — leave the white part of the rind behind.

Lemon, lime, orange, and grapefruit juices. Any of these is nice in ginger ale or in all-citrus drinks. Keep adding fruit to your water-sugar mixture until the taste is right. Yeasts work much more slowly in a relatively concentrated batch of citrus drink. To help keep the yeast from giving up altogether, agitate the drink vigorously as you are making it, and just before and after you add the yeast. The oxygen you force into the liquid will help keep the yeast contented. Consider adding an additional ingredient as a yeast nutrient — perhaps a little malt extract, or some warm water in which chopped raisins have been steeping.

Lemon Beer

Recipe of Daniel Young
Canada, 1861

To make 20 gallons, boil 6 ounces of ginger root bruised, ¼ lb. cream-tartar for 20 or 30 minutes in 2 or 3 gallons of water; this will be strained into 13 lbs. of coffer sugar on which you have put 1 oz. oil of lemon and six good lemons all squeezed up together, having warm water enough to make the whole 20 gallons, just so you can hold your hand in it without burning, or some 70 degrees of heat; put in 1½ pint hops or brewer's yeast worked into paste as for cider, with 5 or 6 oz. of flower; let it work over night, then strain and bottle for use. This will keep a number of days.

Raspberry Shrub

Recipe of
Mrs. Julia Howitt
United States, 1902

Place raspberries in stone jar, cover with good cider vinegar, let stand over night; next morning strain and to one pint of juice add one pint of sugar; boil ten minutes; bottle while hot; use about one-half glassful of shrub to one-half glassful of pounded ice and cold water. Delicious drink for summer.

Raisins. Raisins add a rich, fruity flavor to any soft drink recipe. In the old days they were added not only for their flavor, but also because they were high in both tannins (which help prevent cloudiness in beverages) and natural yeast. To extract the flavor, chop the raisins, then pour a pot of hot water over them and allow to steep. Strain after an hour or two, discarding the raisins. Don't use hot water if you want to utilize the natural yeasts of organically grown raisins. One way to use raisins is simply to drop one or two in each bottle at bottling time — many old-timers did this no matter what kind of drink they were making. Also experiment with dried currants, sultanas, figs, dates, apricots, apples, peaches, and pears.

BARK, TWIGS, AND SAP

The bark of trees is an important source of flavor in a number of types of beverage recipes. Sap replaces part or all of the water in a recipe, and also provides sweetness, flavor, and aroma. Bark, twigs, and sap all provide vitamins, minerals, and other nutrients. Many contain active ingredients useful in herbal medicine.

Cinnamon bark. The curly sticks of cinnamon bark are readily available in all supermarkets. One to 6 inches per gallon of soft drink should be enough for most recipes — with this spice, a little goes a long way.

Wild black cherry bark. This tree *(Prunus serotina)* grows over nearly all of eastern North America and as far west as the Dakotas and Arizona. Its bark is a traditional root beer ingredient, and herbalists credit the bark with helping coughs and colds, as well as being a mild sedative. Don't overdo wild black cherry bark; the flavor is not unlike that of stale cigars. *Note:* The bark should be steeped in hot water, not boiled.

Spruce twigs. I can't say this is one of my favorites, but spruce beer was an American tradition in many areas of the country. Others do seem to enjoy the taste, and colonial brewers appreciated the preservative qualities of spruce, especially when hops were not readily available. Experiment with 1 pint of spruce twigs for 1 gallon of soft drink. The best-tasting spruce is black spruce *(Picea mariana)*; certain other species of spruce yield an unpleasant, musky flavor. Oil of spruce is available at drugstores; the historical recipes included in this volume attest to the fact that it was quite commonly used in place of spruce twigs in early American kitchens.

Birch, sweet birch, or black birch *(Betula lenta)*. Trees can be tapped in early spring, much as maple trees are tapped as winter ends. Use birch sap in place of water in making soft drinks to give a slight wintergreen flavor. The sap will also contribute a modest natural sweetness. Several handfuls of the twigs of sweet birch add flavor to any beverage, and the twigs are richer in wintergreen aroma than is the sap. Traditional "birch beers" also had sassafras in the recipe; take care to allow the birch flavor to come out by using only a moderate amount of sassafras. (For instructions for tapping trees, see Appendix B.)

Maple sap. Both root beers and beers can be brewed with maple sap instead of water. Maple sap is so much more dilute than maple syrup that the resulting beverage does not taste much like maple syrup — the taste is crisp and clean. (Appendix B includes a discussion of tapping trees.)

Oil of wintergreen. Available in most drugstores, oil of wintergreen gives a flavor similar to that of birch twigs to any root beer. Try ¼ teaspoon per gallon of root beer.

Wild wintergreen leaves. Drop two little wintergreen leaves in each bottle of a soda for a little extra flavor. Don't attempt to build a recipe around this plant — you would almost certainly have to over-collect to get enough for a hefty wintergreen taste.

SWEETENERS

It is really fairly easy to keep yeasts happy. As long as they are in a watery solution that is neither hot nor cold, they are cheerfully active — that is, as long as they have something to eat. Every recipe must contain some form of sugar for the yeasts to consume. With beers and wines, the yeasts are converting sugar to alcohol. In the case of soft drinks, we want the yeasts to convert the sugars to a tiny (unnoticeable) amount of alcohol. A pleasant level of carbonation is a byproduct of this conversion.

Corn sugar. Those who brew beer at home routinely use this sugar in their recipes, and they soon learn to disdain regular table sugar. Corn sugar *is* preferable to table sugar in the full-scale fermentation undergone by beers, which require a second fermentation once bottled. For the quick fermentation that soft drinks go through, though, corn sugar offers no noticeable improvement to the recipe. You will save money by sticking to table sugar.

Birch Beer

Recipe of a Fair Lady England, 17th Century

To every *Gallon of Birch-water* put a quart of *Honey,* well stirr'd together; then boil it almost an hour with a few *Cloves,* and a little *Limon-peel,* keeping it well scumm'd. When it is sufficiently boil'd, and become cold, add to it three or four Spoonsful of good *Ale* to make it work . . . and when the *Test* begins to settle, bottle it up . . . . It is gentle, and very harmless in operation within the *body,* and exceedingly sharpens the *Appetite,* being drunk *ante pastum.*

Test: Yeast

Ante pastum: Before a meal

Molasses Beer

Recipe of Miss Leslie
Published at
Philadelphia, 1853

To six quarts of water, add two quarts of West Indian molasses; half a pint of the best brewer's yeast; two table-spoonfuls of ground ginger; and one table-spoonful of cream of tartar. Stir all together. Let it stand twelve hours, and then bottle it, putting three or four raisins into each bottle.

It will be much improved by substituting the juice and grated peel of a large lemon, for one of the spoonfuls of ginger.

Molasses beer keeps good but two or three days.

Honey. This ingredient can subtly modify the flavor of soft drinks when used to replace all or part of the refined sugars. Even more subtle variations are possible by experimenting with a variety of honeys, such as clover honey, basswood honey, and orange blossom honey. Honey is sweeter than table sugar, so try substituting ¾ cup of honey for 1 full cup of sugar.

Maple syrup. Use only genuine maple syrup. The inexpensive brands are mostly corn syrup and artificial flavoring. Consider using 2 cups or a bit more for 1 gallon of soft drink, with no additional sugar.

Molasses. Not everyone likes molasses, but this is an ingredient that — used in moderation — adds a rich, buttery taste to any bottled beverage. It has the added advantage of coloring the drink; if you want a brown root beer, even a small amount of molasses will give it to you. Start with only a tablespoon or two per gallon, and gradually add more molasses to taste. If you are sure you like molasses flavor, you may want to use ¼ cup or more per gallon. The various types of molasses and related products available include light, dark, and black-strap molasses, and sorghum and ribbon cane syrup. No matter which kind you use, though, the best idea is to add slowly, tasting as you add the syrup.

Artificial sweetener. If you must cut sugar to the bare minimum in soft drinks, you can turn to artificial sweeteners, adding the *equivalent* of 1¾ cups of sugar per gallon of drink. The package will give you information about equivalency. You must also add 4 tablespoons of table sugar per gallon of drink to allow the yeast to carbonate the beverage. Artificial sweetener is not fermentable, and without some real sugar in it your beverage will be entirely flat. I can't say I'm enthusiastic about this ingredient.

HERBS AND SEEDS

This section includes leaves, many of which are routinely used in the making of teas. The same kind of infusion process that works for tea can also be used to make a batch of soft drink.

Coriander seed. Before the development of hops as a beer additive several centuries ago, coriander was a popular beer flavoring. Even today, a style of beer called Belgian white beer uses coriander seed and orange peel as the flavoring agents, together with spicy hops. I have never heard of anyone using coriander in soft drinks, but stranger things have happened.

Hops. A variety of hops is available, ranging from spicy (Saaz), to citrusy (Cascade), to flowery (American Tettnanger). For adding bitterness, the varieties are essentially interchangeable; you either use a little of a very bitter hop or twice as much of a hop that is half as bitter. Hops impart an interesting flavor to ginger ales and are found in some root beer recipes as well.

Lemongrass. Native to Southeast Asia, this plant is now cultivated all over the world for its pleasant lemon taste. It's a good way to give a lemony boost to any soft drink, because lemongrass will not slow down fermentation as lemon juice will.

Mint leaves. Spearmint or peppermint can be a nice ingredient in ginger ale or citrus soft drinks. Simply make a tea of the mint leaves and add it to your other ingredients. You could even make medicinal soft drinks: Study herbals, and make use of horehound, catnip, selfheal, and other potable members of the mint family. *Caution:* As always, be sure to consult field guides and develop a certain expertise before using any unfamiliar plant for food or drink.

Star anise. Native to the southern United States, this is a nice ingredient for those who like its distinctive taste. Star anise may be used in conjunction with licorice root, since licorice candy has the flavor of both licorice root and anise. Use ¼ to ½ ounce per gallon of soft drink.

Vanilla bean. Vanilla bean is not cheap, but even a 2-inch piece will add a noticeable richness to a gallon of soft drink. For a stronger vanilla flavor, consider using 4 or 5 inches. If vanilla bean is not available, you can substitute vanilla extract. Avoid boiling the extract; instead, simply add it after the boil is complete.

Wild sarsaparilla *(Aralia nudicaulis).* Also called small spikenard, this plant grows over much of eastern North America and as far west as Manitoba and Colorado. It is a traditional root beer plant, and herbalists describe its diuretic and stimulant properties. Several Native American tribes made a cough medicine from this plant's roots. Three or 4 ounces of dried root in a recipe containing other roots should be about right.

Yarrow leaves *(Achillea millefolium).* In olden times, Swedish brewers used the leaves of this common wildflower instead of hops. This is one of many ingredients on my list to try.

Yellow dock, curled dock *(Rumex crispus).* The old herbals called yellow dock a "blood purifier," and many still regard it is a healthful tonic. Many old root beer recipes use yellow dock as a primary ingredient. Try a small root or two (fresh or dried) in a gallon of root beer, though don't expect it to add much flavor or color.

VARIOUS EXTRACTS, ESSENCES, AND OILS

On the shelf next to the vanilla extract in any large supermarket you will find an enticing array of extracts, all waiting to be incorporated into your latest carbonated creation. Try extracts of almond, anise, black walnut, lemon, maple, orange, peppermint, pineapple, and spearmint. Old-fashioned drugstores like the ones in my hometown have bottled oils and essences including sassafras, wintergreen, and spruce. Wine-making suppliers also sell concentrated flavorings for cordials, and these flavorings also work well in soft drinks. You could build recipes for soft drinks that mimic the flavor of cordials, such as Chartreuse and benedictine, but without the alcohol content.

COFFEE

There are two ways to use coffee in soft drink recipes. One is to use fresh-made coffee in place of all or part of the water. The other is to add fresh-ground coffee directly into the jug or carboy and allowing the liquid to steep (try ¼ pound of ground coffee per 2 gallons of beverage). Never boil the ground or liquid coffee in your recipe.

Other Ingredients to Try

- Allspice, whole
- Apple juice
- Bergamot
- Black tea
- Chocolate
- Cloves
- Grape juice
- Herbal teas
- Juniper berries
- Nutmeg
- Pawpaws
- Persimmons
- Prickly pears
- Pumpkin
- Raspberries
- Tomatoes

Making Minor Adjustments

In developing soft drink recipes, the secret is to move slowly, adding ingredients and tasting repeatedly. (If you are brewing the drink on the stove top, be sure that all the water has been added before you begin the tasting, or at least compensate in your mind for the fact that all the water is not yet present.) If a mixture tastes good in its uncarbonated state, it will taste good as a finished soft drink. When you are trying a new idea, you may want to make a small batch — say, a half gallon. This way, if the drink is a complete disappointment, at least the amount of ingredients you've wasted will be minimal.

Collecting Plants

The fun of making homemade beverages from scratch is enhanced considerably when you gather some of the ingredients yourself from the wild. Most plants that yield a nice juice or tea can also produce a good soft drink. Many of the plants listed in this chapter can be gathered in the wild, though the list is biased in favor of the eastern United States and Canada. Readers who live in other areas should experiment with the edible plants they are familiar with. *Caution:* Be sure to use a reliable field guide and develop a certain expertise before making drinks from wild plants.

In a too often fouled world, you may need to think about the safety of eating what you collect. If you collect plants that are growing in standing water, consider the quality of the water. Is it in an industrial area — or fouled in some other way? Similarly, although it is very easy to locate plants growing next to the road, you should pause and think about the amount of tailpipe emissions that may have settled on these plants.

If you are a city-dweller, you may be tempted to gather plants in parklands, but to avoid spending the night in the lockup, be sure to follow the park rules. Reasonable collecting is permitted on most national forest lands, but any is prohibited in national parks. State parks have a variety of rules, usually set out in the printed visitor's guide. To collect on private property, be sure to secure the landowner's permission. In all cases, be a good citizen: Pack out all trash, and fill in carefully any holes that you dig.

After collecting a certain plant once or twice in a year, move on to another kind of plant as an added way of ensuring that you do not over-collect. By being a thoughtful, prudent collector of plant materials, you increase the likelihood that the plants will be here for the next generation.

Troubleshooting

Making a bad batch of soft drink is a discouraging experience. The degree of disappointment is usually proportional to the amount of time and money you have invested. You will probably shed few tears over a funny-tasting gallon of root beer you've made from extract. On the other hand, it can really ruin your day to take that first sip of your 5-gallon batch of crab apple soda, made from fruits laboriously gathered on three successive afternoons, only to realize that it has the taste of chopped cardboard.

Bad batches really are of two kinds. One is caused by a misguided recipe or an important mistake with the ingredients. The other kind of bad batch comes from a failure in sanitation, whereby the beverage is "infected" with wild yeasts, bacteria, or other microorganisms.

Tomato Beer

Mrs. M. E. Porter
Virginia, 1871

A VERY healthy and palatable beer can be made in this wise: Gather ripe, sound tomatoes; mash, strain through a coarse linen bag, and to every gallon of juice add one pound of good, moist brown sugar; let it stand nine days; pour off and bottle closely; the longer kept the better. When used, fill nearly full a pitcher with sweetened water, add lemon juice to suit taste, and to this some of the preparation described, and you will find it equal to the best lemonade. To half a gallon of sweetened water add one tumblerful of beer.

As the number of acres of wild and undeveloped land decreases every year, a word about the justice of collecting seems in order. Before collecting any wild plant, take note of how common it is in the area. If you find a dense thicket of sassafras saplings, there can be little harm in digging one or two. The late Euell Gibbons reported the folk wisdom that for every sassafras you dig, two more will come in its place. If you find a cow pasture full of burdock, the cows would undoubtedly be grateful to you for digging some. If, on the other hand, you find only a lonely specimen or two of wild peppermint, it would be the better part of valor to leave it be.

The way to prevent the first kind of failed batch is to use a trusted recipe, or to move away from trusted recipes only slowly. For example, if you like the Three-Root Root Beer (see page 46), but would like more licorice flavor, move from 2 teaspoons of licorice root to 3 — don't jump immediately to 8 or you may see your friends and family grimacing at the latest concoction. Also, exercise a certain amount of care, double-checking your recipe as you go. It's always disappointing to realize that you just added 1 pound of sugar, for example, when the recipe actually called for 1 *cup*. (It's just as disappointing to forget to add the sugar altogether!)

Remember, too, that you are working with natural ingredients that vary in their traits from batch to batch. Dried roots and leaves can lose their flavor; some limes may lack in tartness; molasses can go musty. Your best bet is to avoid relying *exclusively* on a recipe, and plan to use your senses of sight, smell, and taste. With a little experience you will be able to discern that a batch of root beer you're about to bottle is far too weak in taste and color, or that your lemon soda is outrageously sour and needs more water and sugar.

A problem with relying on taste, aroma, and color is that with most of the recipes in this book, only half of the water goes through the boiling or steeping process; the rest of the water is added plain. This means that the liquid you will be evaluating for taste, smell, and color will be at double strength, and you will have to do some mental arithmetic to compensate for the water that will be added later. The reason the recipes do not boil or steep all the water with the flavorings is that contamination with wild yeasts and other unwanted lifeforms becomes a real possibility when sugary liquids are allowed to sit at room temperature. Thus, the recipes in this book cool the hot liquid very quickly by adding them to a large amount of cold water. This way the beverage is at lukewarm temperature for only a few minutes before it is safely in bottles.

If you find it too trying to taste a double-strength beverage in the pot and predict how it will taste as a finished product, there is another route you can take. This method is so simple and works so well that I am heartily ashamed to admit that I had been making beverages for several years before I thought of it. When your wort is nearly finished simmering, take a tablespoonful of the wort and put it in a teacup. Then add a tablespoon of cold water. Voilà! The contents of this teacup should taste delicious. The sweetness should be just right (or a *tiny* bit sweeter than you want, since a small amount of sugar will be consumed by the yeast as carbonation occurs). The flavor should be just the way you want it — the process of carbonation and aging isn't going to improve a bad flavor or a weak one. If the flavor is too strong, add more water and taste again. If it is too weak, add some more of your flavoring ingredients. If the beverage isn't sweet enough, add more sugar and taste again. If the beverage is too sweet, you can add more water, but be sure to taste again; the flavors may now be too weak.

COMMON PROBLEMS WITH HOMEMADE SOFT DRINKS

Gushing bottles. The drink was allowed to sit too long at room temperature. To cope with the overcarbonated batch you now have on hand, make sure the drinks have been thoroughly chilled in the refrigerator before opening. (Chilled drinks are less likely to gush, or will gush less severely.) Try opening over the kitchen sink, prying the cap only a little at a time. It may take 15 minutes to open the bottle, but at least the drink won't be wasted.

To prevent this happening with future batches, try one or more of the following approaches. After bottling, let the bottles sit for less time at room temperature, or move them to a cooler place. Check a single bottle as soon as 36 hours after bottling, especially if the room is quite warm. When the carbonation is right, immediately put all bottles into the refrigerator, or any other very cold place that is above freezing. Drink all of the beverage within four or five weeks of storing it in the refrigerator.

In some cases, gushing bottles may be caused by a failure in sanitation (see "This drink tastes terrible!" below).

Exploding bottles. Read the section on gushing bottles, since this is really the same problem (overcarbonation) in its advanced stages. In most cases, bottles break only when you are trying to store homemade soft drinks for a period of months, or at a temperature warmer than a refrigerator keeps.

Weak carbonation. This problem results from moving the bottles into a cold location before they are sufficiently carbonated. Leave the bottles at room temperature until the carbonation is strong enough. Remember that recipes calling for a large amount of citrus juices will work very slowly, taking a week or more, in most cases, to develop the carbonation.

If only one bottle has weak carbonation, you probably have experienced a leaking bottle cap. Make sure your caps are of high quality and are properly attached to the bottle. Check to see that the top of the bottle itself is not rough or broken. Also (as I have learned from bitter experience), never use cork-lined bottle caps.

No carbonation. This usually means the yeast was never active. (You did add the yeast, didn't you? And the sugar?) Be sure the beverage is lukewarm before you add the yeast; higher temperatures can kill yeast. Another possibility is that your yeast was of poor quality — was it a cheap yeast, with no name on the package? Did you use a package of yeast that had been open in your refrigerator for two years? Get some new high-quality yeast.

See "Weak carbonation" above; some of those suggestions may prove useful for drinks that have no discernible fizz.

"This drink tastes terrible!" First consider the recipe. Does it contain dubious ingredients, or strange quantities of ingredients? Asparagus soda is a logical possibility, but most drinkers would object to the taste. Did you neglect to add an ingredient, or did you get an amount wrong?

Off-tastes may also occur because of a lack of sanitation. Scientists can identify by Latin name the microbes that cause each of the common off-odors or off-flavors in beers and soft drinks. Still, such precise identification really isn't necessary since the remedy for almost all such unpleasantness is the same: better sanitation. Among the odors and flavors commonly associated with "infections" of the wort are butterscotch or buttery; sulfur or rotten eggs; rubbery, cooked vegetable; and general sourness. Once you have experienced a bad batch, a massive cleanup of every bottle, jug, carboy, pail, and utensil you own is in order. This should include a scrubbing as well as a soak in a sanitizing solution such as water and chlorine bleach.

One off-odor that may not be caused by infection of the wort is a skunky smell, which is sometimes caused by jugs or bottles of beverage having been exposed to light. Brown bottles are more resistant to this problem than are green, and green are more resistant than clear. The best solution is to store all bottled drinks — and all filled jugs and carboys — in a dark place.

"This drink looks bad." Something floating in the drink is probably pulp, bark, or some other natural ingredient. If this bothers you, next time strain the drink before bottling. These same comments hold true for a mass of assorted material at the bottom of the bottle. Here, though, careful pouring can keep the material out of your glass, if you especially want to avoid drinking it. If the sediment is thin, whitish, and uniform, it is simply yeast, and you should learn to live with it. Once again, careful pouring will keep the yeast out of your glass if you'd prefer not to drink it.

Those who are experienced in making homebrewed beers know that one telltale sign of an infected batch is a ring around the neck of the bottle. While such a ring may also mean your soft drink batch has been spoiled by bacteria or other unwanted nasties, you should recognize that with soft drinks such rings can also be caused by bits of root floating to the top of the bottle, or by floating bits of citrus pulp. Thus, taste will be a better indicator of a bad batch than any ring around the neck of the bottle. Whatever caused the ring, though, be sure to clean the bottle with a bottle brush and then soak in a solution of water and chlorine bleach before brewing again.

chapter 7

Ensuring Variety

hen I was in college I kept a poetry notebook into which I scribbled all kinds of stuff, especially late at night. One evening in 1978 I wrote this:

> *I want to loose myself*
> *From strictures of fact.*
> *I want to leap to other towns,*
> *Sip strange beverages.*

Yet another entry that didn't look quite as good by the cold light of the next day! But it is interesting that some two decades later, having leapt to Buckhannon, West Virginia, I am still working to avoid boredom in the liquid refreshment department. I have now made several dozen different traditional and nontraditional brewed soft drinks, and after making several dozen more I may begin to run out of ideas.

New Directions with Old Favorites

There is a great variety of nonalcoholic, nonbottled, noncarbonated beverages. Most Americans focus on two: tea and coffee. Even in these narrow categories there are more than a hundred variations. Hot or iced? Caffeinated or decaffeinated? With sugar or without? With milk or black? In the case of coffee, there are the oily African varieties and the aromatic products of South America and Arabia. Some specialty stores even sell coffee beans that have been flavored with extracts of chocolate, almond, raspberry, or orange. A blend of coffee and chicory is marketed as New Orleans–style coffee, while a blend of coffee and piñon nuts is made in New Mexico. If you purchase a special coffeemaker, you can add to your repertoire such delicious drinks as espresso, cappuccino, and café con leche.

In the case of tea, there is the wonderful Earl Grey variety, made from a mixture of tea and an oil derived from the fruit of the bergamot plant (a member of the mint family). You can also choose from among black tea, green tea, orange pekoe tea, and spider leg tea. The latter tea, fortunately, is named for the shape of the dried leaves. Then there is oolong tea, an Oriental tea that is fermented before it is dried. Add in commercially purchased or locally gathered herb teas, and the possibilities really begin to multiply. Finally, don't forget the various hot grain beverages marketed as coffee substitutes, under brand names including Postum, Pero, and Caffix. These are creamy and, to my taste, very good. Or make your own hot drink mixes, experimenting with chicory, malt extract, molasses, and spices.

Hot chocolate drinks are enjoyed around the world, often with more of a water base than the milky beverage consumed in the United States. Here, then, are additional possibilities: milk-based hot chocolate, water-based hot chocolate, cinnamon hot chocolate, hot chocolate with vanilla, and hot chocolate topped with marshmallows.

By partaking of all the varieties of coffee, tea, and cocoa, and the dozens of recipes for bottled soft drinks given earlier, plus the additional recipes you'll find in this chapter, you could easily enjoy a different potable experience every day of the year. The opportunities to "sip strange beverages" (in the best sense) are nearly limitless. This chapter closes out the book by offering recipes for nonbottled beverages.

Those who want to re-create the traditions of colonial America could brew Persimmon Beer or Cornstalk Beer. Those interested in the folklore of West Virginia and Kentucky can collect an array of root beer recipes from people living in the hills and hollows. But what recipes will those living in the twenty-second century turn to when they want to partake of the drinks their great-great-grandparents enjoyed? Undoubtedly blender drinks.

We'll start this last section of recipes with several blender drinks. To those who had hoped this book would stick to traditional beverage-making methods of the past and not stray off to traditional beverage-making methods of the future, I will say that a wire whisk — or even a slotted spoon and a strong arm — can work wonders with these same recipes. From blender drinks we will move on to several punches and coffee drinks, then end up with one last look at fizzy drinks.

Coffee Whizzer

This is a fun drink because the milk actually whips, forming a nice layer at the top of the glass not unlike whipped cream — but with less fat content. Also, you get to watch the interesting phenomenon of a darker liquid slowly "raining" down toward the bottom of the glass. In short, this is an active beverage visually and a rich drink gustatorially.

1 pint cold coffee (brew, then chill)
½ cup whole milk
2 teaspoons sugar

Put all three ingredients in the blender and mix on the "whip" speed for about 45 seconds. Pour quickly into clear glasses. This may be made with regular or decaffeinated coffee, as desired. Milk with reduced fat does not work very well.

 Two servings

Fruit Smoothie

3 cups orange juice
2 ripe bananas
10 ice cubes

Place all ingredients in the blender and mix until the ice cubes are reduced to very fine granules. The consistency will be that of a daiquiri or the "icy" drinks sold under various names in convenience stores. Unlike those drinks, however, this one is good for you!

Variations: Add about 10 stemmed strawberries or ½ cup of raspberries. Or add ¼ cup of creme of coconut (found in the supermarket with cocktail mixers), and/or half a fresh pineapple (peeled).

 Two large servings

Strawberry Yogurt Smoothie

2 cups fresh strawberries, or 16 ounces frozen
unsweetened strawberries
2 ripe bananas
1 cup plain or vanilla yogurt
1/2 cup milk
2 tablespoons sugar, honey, or molasses

Place all ingredients in blender and blend on medium speed until mixture is uniform. Serve immediately.
Variations: Replace the strawberries with blueberries or raspberries.

 Two servings

Simple Eggnog

In this recipe the vanilla extract replaces the traditional rum. Rum extract may be substituted for the vanilla extract if desired. Use of milk with reduced fat will result in a beverage — surprise! — that is less rich.

2 eggs
2 cups whole milk
2 teaspoons vanilla extract
4 tablespoons sugar
Dash salt
Fresh grated nutmeg, for garnish

The traditional method is to whip together all ingredients and serve topped with grated nutmeg. This time-honored approach should, however, be modified given the dangers of salmonella from uncooked eggs. A slow cooking on the stove top will suffice; just make sure you stop before the eggnog turns to pudding! Serve warm, or chill in the refrigerator.

 Two servings

Sherbet Punch

4 sprigs of spearmint
4 cups orange juice
4 cups pineapple juice (unsweetened)
Juice of 1 lemon
Juice of 1 lime
1 quart lime sherbet

Rub the spearmint vigorously in the bottom of the empty punch bowl and discard. Fill bowl with all ingredients and stir gently for a moment. Garnish with additional mint, if desired.

 Six to eight servings

The Orange and Sickle

2 quarts whole milk
3 cups orange juice
½ cup sugar
1 pint orange sherbet

Mix the milk and juice in a gallon jug. Add sugar and agitate until dissolved. Divide sherbet among the glasses, then fill the glasses from the jug. Serve with iced-tea spoons.

 Eight servings

Café Brulot

6 cups strong coffee just out of
the coffeemaker
4 teaspoons fresh lemon peel, zest only
2 sticks cinnamon
1 teaspoon allspice (whole)
5 tablespoons sugar

Mix all ingredients over very low heat for about 10 minutes. Keep heat very low! Strain into coffee cups and serve.

 Six cups

Mocha Java

This recipe is a bit of a bother since it involves making two hot beverages first and then mixing them. The result, however, is worth the effort. This is one of the most heavenly hot drinks there is.

3 cups fresh-brewed coffee
3 cups cocoa, from your favorite recipe
1/2 teaspoon ground cinnamon
Milk and sugar to taste

Mix together the hot beverages and the cinnamon. Serve, adding milk and sugar to taste.

 Six servings

Simple Café Cinnamon

8 coffee cups cold water
Fresh ground coffee (your usual amount,
or try 6 coffee measures)
1 stick cinnamon, 3–4 inches long

Make drip coffee in the usual way, but put the cinnamon stick in the carafe. Let the coffee sit on the warmer for about 10 minutes, but don't overheat it.

Five Variations: Other Simple Flavored Coffees

1. Replace the cinnamon stick with 2 inches of fresh vanilla bean.
2. Put 3 tablespoons of cocoa in the coffee basket with the ground coffee; put cinnamon, vanilla bean, or neither in the carafe as desired.
3. Make coffee (plain, or flavored with cinnamon and/or vanilla), then add ½ teaspoon molasses per cup when served.
4. Make coffee as usual (no cinnamon, vanilla bean, cocoa, or molasses), then add 1 teaspoon of extract to the carafe before serving (vanilla extract, orange extract, rum extract, anise extract).
5. Take a dozen wild hazelnuts and shell them. Crush the nutmeats with a spoon, and put into a 1-pint Mason jar that has 6 coffee measures of ground coffee in it. Allow to sit 24 hours, shaking occasionally. Then put the coffee and the nutmeats into the basket. Store-bought filberts will also work — be sure to buy them unsalted!

 Eight servings

Cheap and Quickly Made Beer

Recipe of Mrs. M. B. Moncure
Virginia, 1870

One table-spoonful of ground ginger, one of cream of tartar, one pint of yeast, one pint of molasses, and six quarts of cold water, let it stand until it begins to ferment, which it will in a few hours, then bottle and set in a cool place, in six hours it will be fit for use.

Drinks from the Siphon

This recipe relies on a device sold in kitchen stores and some large department stores. The siphon injects carbon dioxide into water, resulting in quick and inexpensive soda water. (The siphon also made the career of many a slapstick comedian: ". . . and now for a little seltzer in your pants!")

1 quart water
2 quarts fruit juice (orange, grape, pineapple, etc.)
1 carbon dioxide cartridge

Fill glasses with ice and then pour about two-thirds full with the fruit juice. Top off with water from the siphon. What a healthy soft drink!

Siphons can also be used to mix up drinks from soft drink extracts. You will need only a very small amount of extract per glass of drink, perhaps ¼ teaspoon for a tall glass. Sweeten to taste with table sugar or honey.

 About nine servings

The recipes in this book for traditional root beers, bottled carbonated fruit drinks, coffee drinks, blender drinks, switchels, shrubs, fizzes, pops, sodas, nogs, and punches are truly the beginning of almost limitless possibilities. Congratulate yourself that you are making drinks that are better tasting, more reasonably priced, and healthier than anything available in any store on this earth. Above all, remember to have fun in your beverage making! *Salud!*

Suggested Reading

How-to Guides to Beverage Making

Spaziani, Gene and Halloran, Ed. *The Home Winemaker's Companion*. North Adams, MA: Storey Publishing, 2000.

Pollak, Jeanine. *Healing Tonics*. North Adams, MA: Storey Publishing, 2000.

———. *Dave Miller's Homebrewing Guide*. North Adams, MA: Storey Publishing, 1995.

Papazian, Charlie. *The Homebrewer's Companion: The Essential Handbook*. New York: Avon, 1994.

———. *The New Complete Joy of Homebrewing*. New York: Avon, 1991.

Proulx, Annie, and Lew Nichols. *Cider: Making, Using & Enjoying Sweet & Hard Cider*. North Adams, MA: Storey Publishing, 2003.

General Guides to Plants

Audubon Field Guide to North American Trees. New York: Alfred A. Knopf, 1980.

Cleave, Andrew. *Field Guide to Trees of Britain, Europe, & North America*. North Pomfret, VT: Trafalgar Square, 1995.

Elliot, Douglas B. *Roots: An Underground Botany and Forager's Guide. The Useful Wild Roots, Tubers, Corms, and Rhizomes of North America*. Greenwich, CT: Chatham Press, 1976.

Kirkpatrick, Zoe M. *Wildflowers of the Western Plains: A Field Guide*. Austin: University of Texas Press, 1992.

Mohlenbrock, Robert H. *Macmillan Field Guide to Trees & Shrubs*. New York: Macmillan, 1987.

Newcomb, Lawrence. *Newcomb's Wildflower Guide: An Ingenious New Key System for Quick, Positive Identification of Wildflowers, Flowering Shrubs, & Vines*. Boston: Little, Brown, 1977.

Peterson, Roger Tory, and Margaret McKenny. *Wildflowers: Northeastern & North–Central North America*. Boston: Houghton Mifflin, 1975.

Symonds, George W.D. *The Shrub Identification Book*. New York: William Morrow & Co., 1963.

———. *The Tree Identification Book*. New York: William Morrow & Co., 1973.

Books about Food and Beverages

Angier, Bradford. *Feasting Free on Wild Edibles*. Mechanicsburg, PA: Stackpole Books, 1972.

———. *Field Guide to Edible Wild Plants*. Mechanicsburg, PA: Stackpole Books, 1974.

Beach, David R. *Homegrown Hops: An Illustrated How-to-Do-It Manual*. Junction City, OR: David R. Beach, 1988.

Creasy, Rosalind. *Organic Gardener's Edible Plants*. Washougal, WA: Van Patten Publications, 1993.

Densmore, Frances. *How Indians Use Wild Plants for Food, Medicine, & Crafts*. Mineola, NY: Dover Publications, 1974, reprint of 1928 publication.

Gibbons, Euell. *Stalking the Healthful Herbs*. Chambersburg, PA: Alan C. Hood Company, 1989.

Hitchcock, Susan Tyler. *Gather Ye Wild Things: A Forager's Year*. New York: Harper & Row, 1980.

Krochnal, Arnold. *A Field Guide to Medicinal Plants*. New York: Random House, 1984.

Martin, Laura C. *Wildflower Folklore*. Old Saybrook, CT: Globe Pequot Press, 1993.

Riley, John J. *A History of the American Soft Drink Industry: Bottled Carbonated Beverages, 1807–1957*. Washington, DC: American Bottlers of Carbonated Beverages, 1958.

Sturtevant's Edible Plants of the World. Mineola, NY: Dover Publications, 1972, reprint of 1919 publication.

Sources of the Historical Recipes

Excellent Recipes for Baking Raised Bread. New York: Fleischmann Yeast Company, 1912.

Fernald, Merritt Lyndon, and Alfred Charles Kinsey. *Edible Wild Plants of Eastern North America*. New York: 1958.

Gibson, Mrs. Charles H. *Maryland and Virginia Cook Book*. Baltimore: John Murphy and Co., 1894.

Gregory, Annie R. *Woman's Favorite Cook Book*. Chicago: Monarch Books, 1902.

Lacour, Pierre. *The Manufacture of Liquors, Wines, and Cordials, Without the Aid of Distillation. Also the Manufacture of Effervescing Beverages and Syrups, Vinegar, and Bitters*. New York: Dick and Fitzgerald, 1863.

Leslie, Eliza. *Miss Leslie's Complete Cookery. Directions for Cookery, in Its Various Branches,* 51st ed. Philadelphia: H. C. Baird, 1853.

McCulloch-Williams, Martha. *Dishes & Beverages of the Old South.* New York: McBride, Nast, and Co., 1913.

Papers of the American Philosophical Society. February 1771.

Porter, Mrs. M. E. *Mrs. Porter's New Southern Cookery Book.* Philadelphia: J. E. Potter, 1871.

Seely, Lida. *Mrs. Seely's Cook-book: A Manual of French and American Cookery with Chapters on Domestic Servants, Their Rights and Duties, and Many Other Details of Household Management.* New York: Macmillan, 1902.

Simmons, Amelia. *American Cookery, or the Art of Dressing Viands, Fish, Poultry & Vegetables.* Bedford, MA: Applewood Books, 1996. This is a modern printing of the 1796 edition published in Connecticut.

Tyree, Marion Cabell, ed. *Housekeeping in Old Virginia.* Louisville: 1890.

Wolcott, Imogene. *The Yankee Cookbook: An Anthology of Incomparable Recipes.* New York: Coward McCann, 1939.

Young, Daniel. *Young's Demonstrative Translation of Scientific Secrets, Or, A Collection of Above 500 Useful Receipts on a Variety of Subjects.* Toronto: Rowsell & Ellis, 1861.

Appendix A

Sources for Beverage-Making Supplies

The best way to buy beverage-making supplies is from a local dealer. Look in the Yellow Pages under "Beer Homebrewing Equipment & Supplies" or "Winemaking Equipment & Supplies." For those living in rural areas, seeking out mail-order suppliers is the best option.

Ask friends who make beverages for recommendations of suppliers. Look online for homebrew supply sites by typing in "homebrewing supplies" into any major search engine. Join the American Homebrewers Association and get their excellent publication *Zymurgy* — advertisements for suppliers dot the pages.

The American Homebrewers Association and the Brewers Association are connected organizations that promote the practice of craft brewing. BA serves the commercial brewer; as a hobbyist, think about joining AHA. Learn more about both organizations by calling 303-447-0816 or visiting www.beertown.org.

Appendix B

Tapping Trees

Both maple sap and birch sap have traditionally been used in making American soft drinks. Birch sap, in particular, has been used as a sweetener and flavoring in beverages for many centuries. Maple sap is more familiar as the key ingredient of maple syrup, but it too has had traditional uses as a beverage sweetener and flavoring.

First, a word of warning. Raw sap from sweet birch or sugar maple trees is not especially strong in flavor or in sweetness. The maple syrup we are all familiar with is a product made by boiling away 97 percent (or more) of the volume of the maple sap, leaving only a relatively small quantity of extremely concentrated sweetness and flavor. Birch syrup, too, can be made, but only by boiling sap for a very long time to remove most of the water.

On the other hand, you can take heart from the fact that in order to make a beverage from fresh-tapped sap, you will not have to do any long boiling or other processing. The sap is ready to use. Birch sap imparts a faint wintergreen flavor and a modest sweetness to a birch beer recipe. Adding a quart or two of the small twigs of the birch tree will beef up the wintergreen flavor considerably. In the case of maple, you should resign yourself to the fact that the maple drink won't taste much like maple syrup — at least, not unless you go the route of boiling away much of the water. Drinks made from maple sap have a nice, crisp, woodsy taste that you will find delicious; they just don't taste much like concentrated maple syrup.

Maple trees are tapped as winter is giving way to spring. Sugar maple sap rises on those first almost warm days and falls again at night. Some 250 gallons rise per day, so as long as you don't pick on an especially small tree, taking a gallon or two for beverages won't hurt. Maples other than sugar maple yield a tasty sap too, but boast less sugar per gallon. Sweet birch trees are tapped about a month after the maples, in early spring. For both trees, look for specimens that are at least 1 foot in diameter.

Before tapping the tree, find a spile. The spile is the short tube you put into the hole you drill, through which the sap will flow into your bucket. Elder or sumac stalks are the traditional material for spiles, but if you don't mind using modern materials, a piece of ½-inch PVC pipe, 4 inches long, works very well.

Spile

Brace and bit

You will need a brace and bit, with the bit matched to the size of your spile. A ½-inch bit is appropriate for the PVC spile; if you are using elder or sumac stalk, you will just have to hold the spile up to the bits and see which one works best. Other equipment you will need are a drill, a bucket, and several yards of clothesline.

First, drill your hole waist high, about 2 inches deep, and angled somewhat upward rather than parallel to the ground.

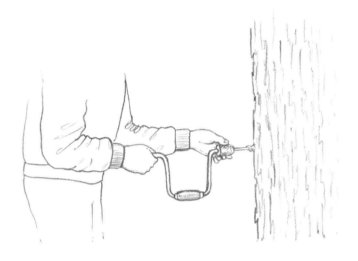

Drilling the hole

When you have drilled the hole, push the spile in, tapping gently with a hammer if necessary, then tie a bucket to the tree with the clothesline. The bucket should be full within 24 hours or so. One good way to improvise a bucket is to use a capped 1-gallon plastic milk jug with a hole cut for the spile. The milk jug will be nearly enclosed, helping to keep out rain and snow, bits of bark, and early insects.

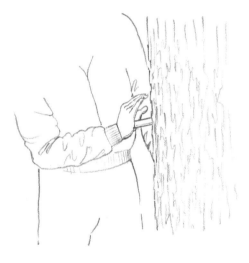

Pushing spile into drilled hole

Both maple and birch sap will ferment readily, so keep the sap refrigerated if you must store it briefly before brewing. Unless you want to experiment with wild yeasts (an uncertain project!), be sure to boil the sap as you are making your beverage.

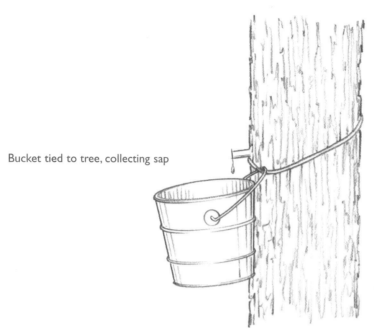
Bucket tied to tree, collecting sap

One way to make your sap stronger in flavor, aroma, and sweetness is to put it in a milk jug and freeze it solid. Next, allow about one-third of the liquid to melt. The sugary liquid will melt before pure water, so if you pour off the melted liquid, the remaining ice will be mostly water. Thus, you should save the melted liquid and discard the ice. If you do this with 3 gallons of sap, you'll have 1 gallon of considerably stronger sap to work with. Another way is to boil water out of the sap on the stove top. After several gallons of water have entered the atmosphere of your kitchen, however, you may notice that the wallpaper is peeling, or the drywall bubbling. The ice method offers a nice alternative to boiling.

Appendix C

Converting Recipe Measurements to Metric

Use the following formulas for converting U.S. measurements to metric. Since the conversions are not exact, it's important to convert the measurements for all of the ingredients to maintain the same proportions as the original recipe.

When the Measurement Given Is	Multiply It By	To Convert To
teaspoons	4.93	milliliters
tablespoons	14.79	milliliters
fluid ounces	29.57	milliliters
cups	236.59	milliliters
cups	.236	liters
pints	473.18	milliliters
pints	.473	liters
quarts	946.36	milliliters
quarts	.946	liters
gallons	3.785	liters
ounces	28.35	grams
pounds	.454	kilograms
inches	2.54	centimeters
degrees Fahrenheit	$\frac{5}{9}$ (temperature − 32)	degrees Celsius (Centigrade)

Index

Page references in *italics* indicate illustrations.

Other Storey Titles You Will Enjoy

Cider, by Annie Proulx and Lew Nichols.
Thorough coverage of every step of cider making, from choosing and planting the best apple varieties to making sweet and hard ciders, sparkling cider blends, and cider-based foods.
224 pages. Paper. ISBN-13: 978-1-58017-520-3.

Cordials from Your Kitchen, by Pattie Vargas & Rich Gulling.
More than 100 easy cordial recipes for delicious, elegant liqueurs for entertaining or gift giving.
176 pages. Paper. ISBN-13: 978-0-88266-986-1.

Dave Miller's Homebrewing Guide, by Dave Miller.
A simple yet complete overview of homebrewing that is clear enough for the novice but thorough enough for the brewmaster.
368 pages. Paper. ISBN-13: 978-0-88266-905-2.

Healing Tonics, by Jeanine Pollak.
Tasty, health-promoting recipes for drinks that can help boost mental clarity, increase stamina, aid digestion, support heart health, and more.
160 pages. Paper. ISBN-13: 978-1-58017-240-0.

The Home Winemaker's Companion, by Gene Spaziani and Ed Halloran.
A guide for all levels, starting with your first batch of kit wine to mastering advanced techniques for making wine from fresh grapes.
272 pages. Paper. ISBN-13: 978-1-58017-209-7.

Making Wild Wines & Meads, by Pattie Vargas & Rich Gulling.
More than 100 recipes to make great wine — with everything but grapes!
176 pages. Paper. ISBN-13: 978-1-58017-182-3.

North American CloneBrews, by Scott R. Russell.
More recipes to duplicate your favorite American and Canadian beers at home.
176 pages. Paper. ISBN-13: 978-1-58017-246-2.

These and other books from Storey Publishing are available wherever quality books are sold or by calling 1-800-441-5700.
Visit us at *www.storey.com.*